MW01006990

GREED
ON TRIAL

GREED
ON TRIAL

Doctors and Patients Unite to Fight Big Insurance

THERESA BARTA

BROWN BOOKS
PUBLISHING GROUP

© 2018 Theresa Barta

All rights reserved. No part of this book may be used or reproduced
in any manner without written permission except in the case of
brief quotations embodied in critical articles or reviews.

Greed On Trial
Doctors and Patients Unite to Fight Big Insurance

Brown Books Publishing Group
16250 Knoll Trail Drive, Suite 205
Dallas, Texas 75248
www.BrownBooks.com
(972) 381-0009

A New Era in Publishing®

Names: Barta, Theresa.
Title: Greed on trial : doctors and patients unite to fight big insurance
    / Theresa Barta.
Description: Dallas, Texas : Brown Books Publishing Group, [2018]
Identifiers: ISBN 978-1-61254-969-9
Subjects: LCSH: Health insurance--Economic aspects--United States. |
    Medicine--Practice--Economic aspects--United States. | Medicine-
    -Law and legislation--United States. | Physicians--Employment--
    United States.
Classification: LCC HG9396 .B37 2018 | DDC 368.382006573--dc23

ISBN 978-1-61254-969-9
LCCN 2017948846

Printed in the United States
10 9 8 7 6 5 4 3 2 1

For more information or to contact the author,
please go to www.GreedOnTrial.com.

To my husband and daughters, who put up with me during the craziest of trials, and to my clients, who stand up and fight for what they believe in—*their patients*.

Greed on Trial is a work of non-fiction based on my own experience as a practicing trial attorney. Except for my own name and the name of my husband, however, I have changed the names and various other identifying characteristics of all individuals and companies who were involved in the cases, including judges, lawyers, doctors, health care companies, witnesses, and litigants. Some of the characters and narrative are a composite based on more than one actual case or person, and some of the dialogue is reconstructed. Any resemblance between the names and other characteristics that appear in my book and real persons is strictly coincidental.

My goal in writing this book is to call attention to a matter of urgent and continuing public concern and debate—our health care system and, in particular, the policies and practices that sometimes interfere with the all-important relationship between doctors and their patients.

Contents

Acknowledgments xi

My Opening Statement 1

A Psychiatrist's Tale

Part I: Doctor and Patient 5

Part II: The Lawsuit 39

Part III: The Trial 57

A Dermatologist's Tale

Part IV: Doctor and Patient 107

Part V: The Lawsuit 137

Part VI: The Trial 163

A Neurologist's Tale

Part VII: Doctor and Patient 193

Part VIII: The Lawsuit 227

Part IX: The Trial 247

Part X: Outcomes 265

My Closing Argument 269

About the Author 273

Acknowledgments

I would like to thank everyone whose support, guidance, and talents made this book possible. My special thanks to Milli Brown, Andy Wolfendon, Katlin Stewart, Cathy Williams, Alex Charest, and Danny Whitworth at Brown Books Publishing, without whom this book would not have happened.

Thank you to my mentors and friends, Dan Schechter, Michael Bidart, and William Shernoff, who taught me to be the trial lawyer I am.

Thank you to each of my clients and their patients, who had the strength, courage, and perseverance to fight back.

And finally, thank you to my husband, Peter, my daughters, Jordan and Lauren, and my parents, without whom I could not do what I do, for their love, encouragement, and support.

My Opening Statement

(How I Became a Doctors' Lawyer)

When I was fresh out of law school, I was hired by one of those mega law firms with a thousand attorneys—the kind of firms that employ the lawyers I always see sitting across the aisle from me in courtrooms these days. It did not take me long to figure out that I belonged at the other table, so to speak—namely *suing*, rather than *defending*, large corporations that put profits ahead of people.

I did gain something precious from my experience at the suit farm, though: insight into how corporate defense attorneys (and their clients) think and into how they litigate cases. That insight has proven itself invaluable to me over the years.

Thanks to one of my law school professors, I eventually switched sides and went to work for a firm that specialized in suing insurance companies. While working there, I represented patients whose insurers refused to pay for vital medical services. This was important and satisfying work, and it taught me a great deal about plaintiff-side law, but something interesting happened during my tenure at this firm. I began to notice that in almost every case, I worked closely with *doctors* as well as patients. That was because it was ultimately the doctors who were not being paid by the insurers.

While working those cases, I realized that doctors themselves were in need of their own advocate. There were plenty of attorneys representing patients, but few standing up for the doctors, who often were victimized by Big Insurance as badly as their patients were.

Eighteen years ago, I started my own law practice and became a physicians' advocate. Since that time, I've represented hundreds of doctors and sued every large insurance company you can think of, as well as many other corporate players in the health-care arena. And thus far—knock on wood—I've been quite successful. My clients have ranged from primary care doctors to specialists of every stripe.

Doctors face many daunting issues with insurers these days, but a common scenario is this: A physician working for a medical group is told to follow some new treatment policy—for example, to prescribe cheaper medications or to double-book patients—so that his or her employer or insurer can save money. The physician, believing the new initiative is not good for patient care, resists the policy, and is then fired and/or "blacklisted" so that he or she can no longer accept insurance.

This scenario occurs with alarming frequency, but most people are not aware of it. Most doctors play ball with the new corporate medical policies because they think they have to—because they think Big Insurance truly is king. When I tell physicians about my practice of suing the large health-care corporations, they say, "I had no idea there were laws that protected us doctors."

There's a lot of misleading and false information out there.

That is why I have written this book. I want doctors to know that they *can* stand up and fight back against the big insurers and medical management companies—and that they can win. (One further thing I've learned from the cases I've tried is that jurors are typically appalled when they find out what insurance companies are doing to doctors these days.)

So beyond just empowering doctors, I also want patients—and we're all patients at one time or another—to know the kinds of pressures their doctors are under. There's a tendency to blame doctors for the "health-care crisis" we're in, because doctors are the frontline people we see and deal with every day. But that's blaming the covictim. It's my experience that most doctors are good, caring, and conscientious professionals who would love to provide the best care possible for their patients, if only they could. But their hands are often tied by policies that are designed to deny and reduce care for patients so that insurers and management companies can increase their profits. I believe that the more patients know about the inner workings of insurance companies and large health-care organizations, the better "armed" they can be as consumers and advocates.

The way I've decided to present my "case" to you is not to lecture on what's wrong with our health-care system but rather to tell you three "true-life" stories. I think a human face is the best way to bring to life the kinds of tragedies that befall real patients and doctors in this brave new world of health-care management by insurance company. The stories you're going to read here are pulled right from my own files. The names and some of the details have been changed, but the cases are largely real. (See the author's note on page vii .)

For each of the three cases, I'll first share the story of a patient and a doctor whose lives and practices spiraled out of control because of arbitrary health-care decisions made by out-of-touch corporate employees. Then I'll show you what happened when I began working the case and making efforts to find the real guilty parties. Finally, we'll take a look at each of the trials and how they turned out for my clients.

As you read these stories, you may find yourself nodding with new understanding and saying, "Ah, so that's why my health-care provider suddenly switched my medication," or "That's why my doctor's office is always so crowded"—or, if you're a doctor, "So that's why my insurance company terminated me." If that kind of recognition dawns, this book will have succeeded. My hope is that, whether you are a doctor or a patient, you will come away from reading this book with a better understanding of how modern health care is being "managed" in ways that serve the bottom line rather than public health. But more than this, I hope you will come away with a sense of *empowerment*. Because here's the great news: you *can* challenge the system . . . and you *can* win.

PART I

A Psychiatrist's Tale

Doctor and Patient

1

Dr. Stephen Han read the sentence a third time, sure he had misread it the first two. "The purpose of this letter is to inform you that your employment with Newton Physicians Group (NPG) will be terminated, effective August 15."

No, he had not misread it. He was being fired. Fired? For the first time in his life? At fifty-eight years of age? Even though he knew he had done nothing "wrong," he felt a sting of shame followed immediately by anger. He needed to walk this off.

"I'll be back in a bit," he told Denise, his receptionist, and shoved open the glass doors of the NPG medical building, a bit more roughly than he had intended. As he strode through the parking lot toward the walkway along the river, he tried to make sense of the shocking news.

Up until the moment he'd read that letter, he had thought he was a valued member of the NPG team and that any issues he had with the administration were minor. As the main psychiatrist on staff at the medical group, he had maintained a busy practice since coming aboard, and he was well liked by patients and staff alike.

Dr. Han had been hired by NPG eighteen months earlier as a "staff physician." He was fifty-six at the time and had been practicing psychiatry for twenty-five years. For many years before that, he had run his own practice with a partner, but when his partner died, Stephen decided to focus solely on treating patients. The NPG staff opportunity was perfect for him. He took a cut in pay, but he gained the stability of a predictable salary and lost the stress of running a business.

Dr. Han had always been a "patient-centric" psychiatrist. His primary focus was on the mental health of his patients, not on making money. His position at NPG gave him the freedom to practice as he saw fit without having to worry about business concerns. For example, he saw several patients from low-income and vulnerable populations on a pro bono basis. The arrangement with NPG had been a mutually positive one.

At least for the first year.

Things had started to change when NPG went into business with a new management company called First Choice. The First Choice administrators implemented a "Drug Cost Savings Plan" and hired a pharmacology PhD named Jim Hirsch to oversee the program. The purpose of the plan—and of the hiring of Hirsch—was to save money on drug costs by "reducing utilizations" by NPG physicians.

But save money for whom? Was this arrangement truly in the patients' best interest? Steve was not shy about asking such questions.

After Hirsch came on board, the parade of memos started. In retrospect, maybe Steve should have taken them more seriously. But they seemed so patently absurd that he assumed they wouldn't gain any traction amongst his fellow doctors.

The first memo had been a general one aimed at all NPG physicians. It called for all patients who were currently taking certain name-brand medications to be switched immediately to lower priced, preapproved generic medications.

Dr. Han tossed the memo into the circular file. You don't just "switch" medications on psychiatric patients; every doctor knew that. Furthermore, he didn't think administrators had any business telling doctors how to treat their patients. So he went on prescribing medication as he had before, using good medical judgment and his patients' needs as his guidelines.

The next memo that came across Steve's desk was addressed to him personally. Its tone was noticeably less cordial than the last one.

That second memo, Steve now understood, was the start of his real trouble . . .

2

Great, thought Karina as she stepped into the waiting area, *a mob scene.* She always felt a bit uncomfortable waiting for her appointment—she didn't like advertising herself as a psychiatric patient—and on crowded days like today, she felt as if the eyes of the world were upon her.

"I have a one o'clock with Dr. Han," she told the receptionist.

"Dr. Han isn't in today. You'll be seeing Dr. Peters."

"Excuse me?" said Karina, sure the receptionist had misspoken. "Who is Dr. Peters?"

"The doctor you'll be seeing today."

Gosh, thanks for clarifying that, thought Karina. "There must be some mistake. I've been Dr. Han's patient for over three years, and I've never seen anyone but him."

"Dr. Han is not in today," repeated the receptionist, with a smile that did not extend to her eyes. "Would you please have a seat?"

Karina sighed and made her way to a freshly vacated chair, snatching up a six-month-old issue of *People* magazine. *This is ridiculous,* she thought. *You don't just substitute one psychiatrist for another.* Psychiatry is not a generic service, like an oil change. Karina had an excellent therapeutic relationship with Dr. Han. She didn't want to see some random person who didn't even know her.

But, of course, she did need to have her meds refilled. And that wasn't going to happen unless a doctor wrote her a prescription. So she was stuck.

She could feel herself "winding up," getting anxious. Then she remembered a calming meditative technique Dr. Han had taught her, and she put it to work. A minute later, she felt relaxed again. *Thank you, Dr. Han.*

For so many things.

She thought back on her time with the doctor, who had, in many ways, saved her life.

Dr. Han had started seeing her toward the end of her first year of college. She'd had a rough freshman year, as many students do. Dr. Han had stepped in and recognized her symptoms as something more than just the "adjustment blues." He diagnosed her with anxiety and depression stemming from an underlying bipolar disorder.

Finding the right medication had been tricky. Dr. Han had led her through a slow, safe process of trial and error. Finally, they'd found the right combination of meds at the right dosages. And Karina had found stability.

Precious stability.

Only those who've lost it know how precious it is.

Karina got her grades under control, completed her next three years of college, and now had her first "real" job as assistant to the PR director of a consulting firm.

The one constant through all of this had been her relationship with Dr. Han. Unlike many psychiatrists, Dr. Han spent *time* with his patients, talking about their lives and struggles, their families, their dreams. And so, when he joined NPG, she'd followed him to his new office. He was her rock.

And now NPG suddenly wanted her to see someone else?

Not going to happen, thought Karina, feeling a sudden surge of rage at the idea. She stood up and stormed out the door.

3

It has come to our attention, *read the second memo to Dr. Steve Han*, that you are prescribing Prozac to several patients. A memo was sent to all physicians in May stipulating that patients be switched to Paxil. We will make an appointment (mandatory) with you to go over the First Choice formulary in the near future. *The memo was signed by Dr. Jim Hirsch and Dr. Adam Wright, Medical Director.*

Now Steve's hackles really went up. He knew how harmful it could be to prescribe only one medication, generically, for all patients, without regard to their specific medical and psychiatric needs. The phrase "one size fits all," he knew, did not apply when it came to prescribing psychiatric medicine.

In Dr. Han's mind, to prescribe a medication on the basis of cost rather than individual medical criteria came dangerously close to malpractice. And so, even after receiving the second memo, he continued to prescribe medication according to his medical judgment and to dodge the administration's attempt to set up a meeting.

This did not fly well in the back office.

At the next physicians' monthly meeting, an unhappy Jim Hirsch announced, "A few physicians continue to prescribe in a manner that places First Choice in a negative fiscal position." Looking only at Steve, he added, "From now on, if a physician prescribes a nonpreferred drug, the physician will pay the difference between the cost of the nonpreferred drug and the cost of the preferred drug."

What? Steve had never heard of such a thing in all of his medical career. He glared at Hirsch and was about to say something sarcastic but decided it might be wiser to bite his tongue. He quietly went back to his practice, kept doing what he had always done, and hoped the problem would go away.

A few days later, Steve received another memo, this one from the medical director. It was a spreadsheet showing that Steve's prescribing pattern was noticeably pricier than all the other NPG and First Choice doctors. The message, though unstated, was clear: We're watching you, and we don't like what we're seeing. Notice how the other doctors are complying.

What Steve wanted to point out was that most of the other doctors were not psychiatrists. The world of psychiatric medication was a delicate and complex one. You had to factor in things like human emotions, thought patterns, relationships, and psychological safety levels. Finding the right medication, or combo of meds, at the right dosage(s) was often the result of much trial and error. Changing to a new medication could cause, at minimum, discomfort for the patient, but it could also trigger major crises, such as psychotic episodes and even suicide attempts. He tried repeatedly to point this out to the administration, but his pleas fell on deaf ears. The mandate stood as written.

A week or two after the physicians' meeting, Steve stepped into the staff lunchroom, where Dr. Patel, a staff neurologist, took him aside and whispered, "Steve, have you seen this? Things have reached a new low." She slipped him an internal memo that made his jaw drop.

First Choice's next planned policy was nothing short of a declaration of war against NPG's doctors and their patients.

4

A few days after storming out of the waiting room, Karina regretted having behaved so impulsively. She was still angry at the NPG staff for scheduling her with a psychiatrist who didn't know her from Emma Watson, but she was out of medication. One thing Dr. Han had drilled into her head was how important it was to stay consistent with her psychiatric meds and to never skip a day.

Swallowing her pride, she called the medical group and asked if she could schedule a new appointment with Dr. Han, ASAP.

"Dr. Han is retired and no longer seeing patients," the receptionist on the phone told her in a blasé manner. "Would you like to see someone else?"

Karina didn't hear the question. She was too stunned. Her heart was pounding in double time. She felt as if the floor was spinning under her feet. How could this be? She had always thought of Dr. Han as family. She couldn't believe he would just stop practicing without telling her. It seemed completely out of character for him.

And didn't physicians have an ethical duty to not abandon their patients?

It had taken her years to develop the working relationship she enjoyed with Dr. Han. Who was she going to see now?

With nowhere else to turn, she called NPG back the next day and asked for an appointment with a new psychiatrist. The receptionist put Karina on hold, treating her to an instrumental version of "Wichita Lineman" that seemed designed to ensure any caller who wasn't already suicidal quickly became so.

A staffer finally came on the line and explained to Karina, "You'll be seeing Dr. Abel, one of our PCPs."

A primary care physician? Why? wondered Karina. She'd been seeing a psychiatrist for years.

"Unfortunately," continued the staffer, "because you'll be classified as a new patient, it's going to take a while to schedule that appointment."

"But I'm not a new patient," Karina protested.

"NPG's policy is that stable and returning patients are graduated back to the PCP team. And when you're first scheduled with a PCP, you are treated as a new patient."

"But I've been coming here for years," Karina insisted.

"Well, because your treatment was terminated and you are requesting it be restarted, you are technically a returning patient."

"*I* didn't leave the practice; my doctor did," Karina tried to argue, but they just went around in circles. The bottom line was that she would have to accept either an appointment with the PCP or nothing at all.

"The closest appointment time we can give you is November 9 at 3:00 p.m."

"But that's three months away!" protested Karina. "I'm out of medication."

"You'll have to discuss that with your new psychiatrist—assuming Dr. Abel refers you to one."

"Can someone give me an emergency prescription?"

"Not without seeing you first." Click.

Three months without medication, thought Karina. *Buckle up, and hold on tight. This is going to be a bumpy ride.*

5

The essence of First Choice's new memo was this:

To support its cost-saving initiative of using only "preferred" medications, First Choice was implementing what amounted to a gag order. Doctors were no longer permitted to talk to pharmaceutical company reps. First Choice was also instituting a "no samples" policy: NPG doctors were no longer to acquire samples of any drugs not on First Choice's approved list. The reason for this was obvious to Steve. First Choice didn't want doctors or their patients to learn about any nonapproved medications, even if they might be beneficial.

Dr. Han felt this policy would tie one hand behind his back. Samples were an essential part of the trial-and-error process he went through with patients. By virtue of free samples, patients—especially low-income and uninsured patients—could try a medication for a week or ten days before they committed financially to a full prescription. And the doctor could fine-tune the dosages.

Dr. Han refused to go along with the new policy. In his view, it was tantamount to withholding treatment and information, which ran counter to the Hippocratic oath. He continued to obtain medication samples privately outside of NPG. He also continued to share information about "nonpreferred" drugs with patients whom he thought could benefit from them. When First Choice denied his patients access to the medications they needed, he filed appeals on their behalf.

The tension between Dr. Han and certain members of the management team continued to escalate, but Steve considered the issue a relatively minor glitch in the grand scheme of things.

That was why the termination letter came as such a shock.

Steve called the HR department to clarify the firing and was told his termination was "without cause." In other words, First Choice didn't want to state the real reason in black and white.

Why not? Steve suspected it was because they wanted to maintain plausible deniability. If he ever decided to make trouble for them, they could say, "There's no evidence he was fired for this reason. He just wasn't a good fit."

Steve didn't intend to fight NPG or First Choice on the firing, but he knew one thing: you only create plausible deniability when you know you're doing something wrong.

6

For the first week without her meds, Karina felt as if she had the flu. She experienced headaches, nausea, a knocked-out feeling. She wished she could stay home from work, but she was still new at her job and felt the need to make a good impression.

After the worst of the physical symptoms passed, the subtler symptoms began to kick in. Lethargy. Trouble sleeping at night. Trouble getting up in the morning. Trouble concentrating at work. Mental cloudiness. "Dark" thoughts.

It was nothing unmanageable, though. At least not yet.

The thought of losing her job was terrifying to her. But she had no one to talk to about her symptoms. Karina was on her own. She decided her only solution was to *will* her way to stability, at least until she restarted her meds. And so far, so good. No major disasters. But the stress of *pushing* herself to remain stable was wiping her out. Her appointment with her new doctor couldn't come soon enough.

Her meeting with Dr. Abel, the primary care physician NPG assigned her, felt as if it was over before it started. In sharp contrast to her experience with Dr. Han, who routinely spent a full hour with his patients, Dr. Abel's session ran about ten minutes. For almost the entire interview, he was looking at a computer, not at her, and firing off questions about side effects and physical symptoms. As she gave answers, he typed notes.

Karina was given no real opportunity to report on how she was doing and feeling. Abel's method seemed so mechanical and impersonal, she assumed he was just asking preliminary questions prior to the start of the "real" session.

So when he stood up, signaling the session was over, she was floored.

"I can't give you the medication you were on before," Abel told her as he walked her toward the door. He didn't explain why. This was a huge blow to Karina. "I *can* put you on a new medication, but it appears you don't really need any medication at all, since you've been med-free for the past three months."

Karina tried to protest that even though she'd been holding it together without meds, it had been really, really rough. Dr. Abel seemed not to hear her. "Why don't we continue without meds for the time being. If you start to feel worse, you can always make another appointment." The door closed behind him.

Karina was deeply dismayed, but she had been raised to believe that the doctor is the expert. As she stepped out of the building, she felt the whole world pressing in on her. She had no idea how she was going to continue coping with the stress of her job without her medication to keep her in balance.

She was angry at Dr. Abel but even angrier at Dr. Han for having put her in this position. Why had he abandoned her like this?

Over the next few weeks, the wheels came off the bus. Karina's mental state started slipping rapidly. She was now lucky to manage two hours' sleep per night, riddled as she was with anxious thoughts. What little sleep she did have was punctuated by nightmares. Each poor night of sleep in turn led to greater stress the next day, as she worried about how she could continue to function. At work, troubling thoughts and images began to intrude on her mind. Before long, she began to spiral into deep depression and started missing work for days at a time.

One day in early December, her roommate came home to an unusually messy apartment and an empty pot burning on the stove.

"Karina?" she called out, more annoyed than worried at that point.

When Karina didn't answer, her roommate pushed her way into Karina's bedroom and found her lying on the floor.

Beside her lay an empty bottle of over-the-counter sleeping pills.

7

Once Dr. Han digested the fact that he really had been fired, his first thought was for his patients. He assumed he would be taking most of them with him when he left. After all, he had brought his patient list with him when he first joined NPG. But how could he continue to see them without an office or a practice? Finding another staff position like the one at NPG would be tough. First of all, he had been fired, and that didn't look good on a resume. Second, he was pushing sixty, and he knew that ageism was real.

He didn't want the headache of starting his own practice at this stage of his life, but that seemed to be his only option.

Starting his own practice turned out to be more stressful and difficult than Steve had anticipated. Not only did he have to refurbish the office space and buy furniture, computers, office equipment, and a thousand other things, but he also had to obtain credentials for private practice and nail down contracts with insurance companies. All of this had to be done quickly in order to avoid a gap in service to his patients.

Setting up the office was expensive and burned through a lot of his savings. His wife, Lucy, agreed to do the billing and office management for free. He was able to hire only one employee—Denise, his receptionist, who agreed to come along with him.

The worst thing was that he ended up losing most of his patients anyway. Some of them could no longer see him for insurance reasons; others just didn't know where to find him.

That was thanks to the way First Choice managed the transition.

When Steve found out he had been fired, he was given four weeks' notice. This was not enough time to personally notify all of his patients, many of *whom he saw only every few months. So he started pulling patients' records and looking for their contact information so that he could notify them in writing. When First Choice discovered he was doing this, they ordered him to stop, saying they would handle the notification of his patients.*

· Steve reluctantly went along with this, trusting First Choice to do the right thing and to follow legal and professional guidelines. That turned out to be a huge mistake.

"Hello," said Steve, grabbing the phone in his deathly quiet new office. "This is Dr. Han."

"Steve, this is Margaret Duffy. I'm a psychiatrist over at—"

"Mercy Medical. Sure, I remember you. How've you been?"

"Good, good. Listen, we've got someone in our ER, a Karina Meyers, who says she's a recent patient of yours. She came in unconscious. Overdose of OTC sleeping pills."

"Oh my God! That's terrible. How is she?"

"We did a gastric irrigation and it looks like she's going to be OK . . ."

"But?"

"Well, she said something I thought you should know about. Evidently, the people at your former employer's office told her that you had retired. I thought that was odd, because I knew you had started your own practice."

"Do me a favor, Margaret. Tell Karina I'll be right there."

8

"Dr. Han?" said Karina, blinking her eyes hard, wondering if she might be hallucinating.

"Karina, I am so sorry this happened to you." Dr. Han explained that there had been a terrible miscommunication and that he had not, in fact, retired, but had started his own practice. She should have been notified about this, he said, and given his new contact information. "But don't worry. I'm going to write up a referral for you to continue to see me outside of your insurance network. For now, let's schedule an appointment for you to see me as soon as you're discharged."

Steve was furious with the NPG / First Choice staff for lying to Karina about his retiring. They could have cost this patient her life. He wanted to explain to Karina exactly what had happened, but he was in a delicate position. He didn't want to tell her he had been fired. Sharing this kind of information with patients can cause them to lose the vital trust and respect they have for their psychiatrist, which, in turn, can compromise their treatment. So he bit his tongue and stuck to the more diplomatic route.

When Dr. Han left her hospital room, Karina burst into tears of gratitude. Although infuriated at NPG for lying to her about Dr. Han, she was thankful that the long nightmare of the past several months was about to end.

And the moment Karina stepped into the waiting room of Dr. Han's new office, she felt as if she were "home" again. She cried throughout the appointment, both relieved and hurt. "You were such a huge help to me," she said. "I just didn't understand how you could leave me like that."

"Again, I can't apologize enough. You should have received a letter telling you that I was leaving and that you had a right to continue seeing me at my new practice. And you should have been given my new address and phone number."

He wrote Karina a prescription for her tried-and-true medication and made a follow-up appointment in three weeks.

Over the next few weeks, several more of Steve's NPG patients trickled into his new practice. They all reported experiences similar to Karina's, saying they didn't know he had opened a new practice and had had trouble finding him. One of them had been told that Dr. Han had "moved away," another that he had "just decided to stop practicing." One of the patients, after asking for Han's new address so she could send him a thank-you card, was told, "Dr. Han doesn't want to have any further contact with his patients." When Steve heard that, he nearly jumped out of his chair.

Steve learned that other patients had been told that they were no longer allowed to see Dr. Han or that he had left NPG because he wanted more money.

Steve was infuriated. Not only was this a huge breach of professional etiquette, but it was also an egregious violation of ethics. Patients had a right to continuity of care. This was especially critical in psychiatry.

Psychiatrists are trained to never abandon patients and to always provide a safe transitional plan in the event they must stop seeing a patient. First Choice was essentially telling Han's patients that he had abandoned them and didn't care about them or their treatment. Steve knew this could lead to some serious, perhaps life-threatening, consequences for his patients—not to mention the harm it was doing to his own reputation. First Choice was not only lying to patients about how and why he left but also denying him access to his patients.

Meanwhile, here he sat on a Tuesday morning, his waiting room empty, listening to the sound of his savings account draining in real time.

He didn't think he could feel any worse.

Until he opened a letter from Karina's health-insurance company.

9

When Karina returned to Dr. Han's office three weeks after her previous appointment, she was excited to be able to report that the meds had started to kick in and that she was starting to feel "normal" again for the first time in months.

But Dr. Han greeted her with a somber look, holding the insurance letter in his hand. "I've got some bad news. Your health-care provider, First Choice, won't approve my request to continue as your doctor. So your insurance won't cover it."

Karina collapsed into her chair with a sigh. "So what are my options?"

"You can go back to NPG to be seen," Han replied, shrugging apologetically. "Or you can continue to see me, but that will have to be an out-of-pocket expense for you."

That was not possible. Karina was earning a low salary at her entry-level job, and she was already paying a heavy premium for her "bronze-level" health insurance plan. Her job didn't offer health insurance, so she had to buy her own policy from a government website. She couldn't afford to pay cash to see a psychiatrist on top of that major expense.

Dr. Han offered to see her at a drastically reduced rate, but it was still more than she could afford.

Steve Han hated the fact that patient care came down to money. He wished he could see patients on a pro bono basis, as he sometimes had at NPG, but now that he was running his own business—a business that was struggling—he needed to produce income during his billable hours. There was no way around it.

And more and more patients nowadays were in the same boat as Karina—bouncing from one doctor to another as their insurance plans changed on an annual basis and each new plan offered its own list of approved providers.

If he tried to see all of these patients for free, his practice would be out of business before it even had a chance to find its footing.

"I'll refill your script for now," he told Karina with a heavy heart, "and I'll give NPG a call to recommend a new psychiatrist for you."

When Karina called NPG to make an appointment with the psychiatrist Dr. Han had referred her to, she was told, again, that it would be a couple of months before she could get in. Dr. Han agreed to see her in the meantime, for no charge.

The day of her appointment with her new psychiatrist finally arrived, and she was shown to an exam room. To her dismay, this wasn't a cozy room with comfy chairs and soft lighting, as Dr. Han had used, but rather a *medical examination* room with harsh fluorescent lighting, a paper-covered exam table, and oxygen tanks.

The "doctor" who came in to see her turned out not to be a psychiatrist; she wasn't an MD at all, but a PA, or physician's assistant. The PA took Karina's blood pressure and said, "So what brings you in today?"

This "doctor" didn't even know why she was here? Karina explained that she was a long-term patient of Dr. Han, coming in for a routine medication consult. "Don't you have my history and a record of my medications?"

"Oh, we've switched over to EMRs, electronic medical records," the PA told her. "It doesn't include any of your paper records from the past. We're starting completely fresh!" She said this as if it were a good thing.

Wonderful, thought Karina. *All the years of painstaking therapeutic work I did with Dr. Han, flushed down the drain as if it never happened.*

After a few very general questions from the PA, the appointment was over.

"What about my medications? I'm almost out."

"I can't prescribe psychiatric medication," said the PA. "It's a company policy that only staff psychiatrists can do that."

"That's who I thought I was seeing! That's why I waited two months for this appointment!"

"I can give you a referral if you want. The front desk can help you schedule that."

Grrrr!

The person at the front desk took Karina's copayment and told her that it would be another four weeks before she could get an appointment with the actual psychiatrist.

"I already waited two months!" Karina said, not loudly but emphatically. The desk person rolled her eyes toward the security officer; the implication was not subtle. "What about my medications?" asked Karina. "I'm almost out."

"That's something the doctor will have to order. I can't help you with that."

"But that's why I scheduled this appoint—oh, never mind! Grrrr!"

The security guard set down his coffee and started ambling toward her, but Karina was already out the door.

10

Karina paced back and forth in her tiny kitchen, trying to work up the nerve to call Dr. Han again. He had never been anything but kind to her, but she felt terrible asking for his help yet again, knowing she couldn't pay him. When she finally had him on the line, she explained what had happened at her appointment and that her meds were going to run out before she could see the new doctor.

"The way they're handling this is ridiculous," Dr. Han told her. "But don't worry about it. I'll call in another refill and see you again for a med review at no charge. But I want you out of their care. I'm going to put in another request for authorization so you can continue to see me."

"That would be wonderful. Thank you, Dr. Han. Is there anything I can do to help speed that process along?"

"Well, it couldn't hurt if you called First Choice and talked to them yourself. They're the ones who have to give approval for one of their patients to be treated elsewhere. Explain to them, in your own words, why it's important for you to keep seeing me."

Steve spent the next two hours writing appeals of requests to First Choice so that he could continue to see some of his former patients from NPG. One of these, of course, was for Karina. He strongly believed she should stay on the "miracle" medication that had kept her stable all these years. He knew that without this medication—which was not approved by First

Choice—there was a strong likelihood that she would decompensate again. That might lead to more suicidal depression, but it might also trigger her entering the "manic" stage of her bipolar cycle. She might begin exhibiting bizarre behaviors and could very well jeopardize her job and her living situation.

First Choice had denied all of his initial requests to see these patients, and now Steve was emphatically appealing those decisions.

For three days running, Karina spent her lunch break trying to track down the name of someone at First Choice she could talk to about getting an authorization to see Dr. Han. Finally, she was connected to a real human being—or a reasonable facsimile thereof.

When Karina explained that Dr. Han's first request for authorization had been denied by First Choice, the woman gave her a response that made her heart sink. "We have no record of any prior requests from Dr. Han."

Karina didn't know what to think of that, but she went on to explain, in detail, why it was important that she continue to see Dr. Han. When Karina was finally finished with her long explanation, the woman said, "We can only give approval for you to see an outside physician if it is determined to be 'medically necessary.'"

"I've just spent ten minutes explaining to you why it *is* medically necessary."

"Only a doctor can make that determination."

"Then why did you just let me talk for ten minutes?"

Click.

11

Karina thought about what the woman at First Choice had told her. Did the office lose Dr. Han's first request to continue treating Karina? Or had Dr. Han lied to her about submitting one? Maybe he was sick and tired of seeing Karina and didn't want to tell her that to her face. She felt a flush of embarrassment.

She made a vow to herself right then and there. Unless she received word from the medical group that she was approved to see Dr. Han again, she would have no further contact with her old psychiatrist. She didn't want to be *that* patient.

Her appointment with Dr. Peters, her newly assigned psychiatrist, didn't go much better than the sessions with the PCP and the PA had. He asked her a generic set of questions and seemed to spend more time looking at his computer than at her. Regarding the medication she had been taking for years—the one that had been so helpful to her—he said, "We don't prescribe that here anymore," and offered to write her a script for something "equally effective, probably even better."

He slid her the prescription face down. When she looked at it, it was for a medication she was already familiar with.

"I tried this one in college, Dr. Peters. It doesn't work for me."

"Our metabolism changes as we grow older," he said. "I really think this is best medication for you." He walked her to the door and said with a casual shrug, "If it doesn't work, just give me a call. We'll get you right in and try something else."

"Ten-five is my best offer," said the car salesman. Steve sighed and handed over the keys. He had thought the 2012 Camry would fetch at least twelve thousand at a dealership, but he was in no position to dicker. He needed the money fast in order to keep his practice open. Selling the Camry was better than selling the house. It was bad enough that he'd already taken out an equity-line-of-credit loan.

When he turned to follow the salesman inside, he noticed a familiar figure eyeing a new Mercedes: Dr. Alvin Supino, a psychiatrist colleague on staff at a local hospital. Steve looked away, hoping he wouldn't be spotted.

"Steve Han," Supino called out. "Say, I heard a rumor. Is it true? Did those bastards at NPG really fire you? Things have really changed over there, haven't they?"

Steve didn't want to lie to a colleague. "Yeah, Al, we had a parting of the ways," he said, and tried valiantly to frame his firing as a blessing in disguise. It was important that Steve remain in good standing with his colleagues. The local psychiatric community was a tight-knit one. They regularly referred patients to one another. And Steve was going to need a lot of those referrals now.

He didn't like the look he saw in Supino's eyes when the two men parted.

Karina finally decided to give the medication Dr. Peters suggested a try. After all, Peters *was* a doctor; there was a remote chance he was right. Maybe the medication *would* work differently this time around.

Well, it sure did. Whereas the pill had had virtually no effect on her the last time she tried it, this time its effect was quite pronounced. Within three days of starting it, she began having intense thoughts of suicide. Worse than ever before.

Doing some online research, she learned that suicidal thinking was a well-known side effect of this medication. *So let me get this straight,* she thought. *People with suicidal histories are routinely prescribed a medication that can actually* cause *suicidal thinking?* Yes was the answer, evidently.

She flushed the medication down the toilet—she didn't want to be on it for another hour—and called Dr. Peters's office for an appointment.

"He can see you two weeks from tomorrow."

"But he said if I was having trouble with my meds, he'd fit me right in."

"That *is* 'right in.' If this is an emergency, go to the ER."

Another two weeks without medication, thought Karina. *Why does this have to be so complicated? Dr. Han already knows what works for me. Why do we have to keep reinventing the wheel and putting* me *at risk in the process?*

12

The day before her appointment with Dr. Peters, Karina had a "revelation"—at least that's what it felt like—that would change her life. Alas, not for the better.

It was the first warm day of spring, and she was walking in the riverside park at lunchtime, as was her habit. Suddenly, she began to feel a spontaneous glow of joy she hadn't felt in years. When two teenagers went whizzing past her on roller skates, laughing, she too began to laugh. She was laughing so hard, she had to sit down in the grass to snap out of it.

An insight arrived, fully formed, in her mind. How she could have missed it before? *The reason I've been taking medication all these years is because I've been depressed. The reason I've been depressed is that I'm tired, lonely, and creatively unchallenged. I don't need* medication, *what I need is to change* those three things. Sitting there in the grass, she quickly worked out a three-pronged plan for self-improvement: 1) Movement. She was going to exercise, dance, and move her body more. 2) Love. She was going to make herself more attractive to men. 3) Creativity. She was going to bring more creativity to her job and her life.

Karina was so excited about her three-pronged plan that she took the rest of the day off. Her first stop was at a sporting goods store, where she bought a $400 pair of inline skates. They cost much more than she could afford, but they were going to be her chief mode of transportation as well as exercise, so she figured *why not go for the best?*

She spent the next few hours at clothing stores replacing her drab, loose-fitting wardrobe. If she wanted to meet men, she needed to embrace her sexuality and stop dressing down. Her new wardrobe cut deeply into her credit card's limit, but this was an important step for her.

Her final stop was at a stationery store, where she bought a beautiful leather-bound "creativity journal" for eighty dollars. She planned to use it to take notes on things that needed changing at her workplace, along with her creative solutions for same.

She capped the day off by canceling her appointment with Dr. Peters. With her three-pronged plan in action, she wasn't going to need meds anymore.

Dr. Han entered his office to find a paper stack of snail mail and a digital pile up of voicemail, but no patients scheduled for the morning. He was on the edge of panic. A few more weeks of business this bad, and he would have to think seriously about closing his doors.

In the mail pile were denials of all of his recent appeals to First Choice, including the one for Karina. There were bills from the office furniture company, the tax accountant, and for the first payment on that home equity loan. Oh, and here was something he hadn't seen since his college days—a blue notice from the power company.

The voicemails were equally distressing. Three of them were from colleagues wanting to know if it was true that he'd been fired. Al Supino must have shot his mouth off, and now everyone wanted to hear the dirt. His reputation was sinking and his self-esteem along with it. Now he was afraid the professional referrals would dry up too.

Also on the voicemail system were distressing calls about two of his other former patients, one of whom was in medical crisis and the other of whom had just been arrested—situations he knew could have been averted if he'd been allowed to continue their care.

The final call was from his wife, Lucy, saying, "You looked terrible when you left here this morning. Are you OK? I'm worried about you."

You're not the only one, *thought Steve. He opened his locking drawer and looked at the stock of drug samples he kept there. For the first time in his life, he wondered what it would be like to swallow a whole handful of them.*

13

Over the next few weeks, Karina worked her three-pronged plan with gusto. She began roller-skating the four miles to work each day. At first, her coworkers cheered her healthy new habit. Their attitudes cooled somewhat when she began trying to organize lunchtime skating sessions for the whole office.

Her change in dress seemed to take everyone by surprise. The day her boss asked her to wear something "more appropriate for the office" was a bit awkward (in a funny way), but overall her new wardrobe was having the desired effect. She was enjoying a major uptick in her sex life. Well, "enjoying" wasn't the *perfect* word—a couple of the guys she'd picked up at O'Leary's turned out to be pretty scary dudes. But what was that expression? You have to kiss a lot of frogs . . .

And creativity-wise, she had become a one-woman wrecking ball for organizational change at work! She was taking the company to brave new places!

That was why the events of May 30 came as such a shock to her.

That morning, Karina decided to skip a mandatory meeting of her department because she decided the project she was working on was more important. It was a project she had initiated herself—a huge collage called "Tolerance and Acceptance" that she planned to hang in the entrance foyer.

Karina was sitting on the floor of her cubicle, cutting pictures out of magazines, when she heard an unfamiliar voice say, "Karina Meyers?"

She looked up to see a man and a woman in police uniforms.

"You're not under arrest, Ms. Meyers," said the policewoman. "We're just going to take you to your doctor's office, where you're going to be evaluated."

Steve was not expecting a call from Wingrove Psychiatric Hospital.

"Dr. Han? We have a patient with us, Karina Meyers, who has identified you as her treating psychiatrist."

Damn, *thought Steve,* I knew she was going to end up in the hospital. *Steve explained that he was no longer officially Karina's doctor, but he consulted with the social worker anyway. After sharing his treatment advice, he suggested that perhaps Wingrove could refer her to him upon discharge.*

There was a pause, and then the social worker came back on the line. "I'm sorry, Dr. Han, but I have a note here saying not to refer any patients to you."

"What?" said Steve, sure he'd heard her wrong. He asked to be transferred to the head of social work, a woman he knew and trusted. When he got her on the line, she confirmed his suspicions: First Choice had told Wingrove not to refer any patients to him.

So I've been blacklisted. This has to stop, *he thought.*

Eight days after her admission, Karina awoke feeling clearheaded for the first time in weeks (perhaps because she was back on the medication that had always worked for her, the one Dr. Han had prescribed), and wondering how the hell her life had come to this. She had been fired from her job, kicked out of her apartment, had three thousands dollars in credit card debt, and was an inpatient at Cedar Grove Psychiatric Hospital.

When the tears started flowing, they just didn't stop.

PART II

A Psychiatrist's Tale

The Lawsuit

14

The first thing that struck me when Dr. Steve Han entered my Newport Beach office was how gentle and nonconfrontational he was. This was not a man driven to make trouble. It was his wife, Lucy, who had persuaded him to meet with me.

After I explained my legal specialty—fighting for doctors who have been retaliated against by insurance companies and medical groups—Dr. Han and I got down to business. Lucy gave me the basics concerning how Steve had been fired by NPG.

"He's been a mess ever since," she said. "He takes it all on his own shoulders, but I keep telling him that *he's* the one who was wronged. He's a good doctor who takes care of his patients, and he was punished for that."

"Why do *you* think you were terminated, Steve?" I asked him.

"I honestly don't know. But in my gut, I don't believe I did anything wrong."

"What reason did NPG give you?"

"None. First they said it was 'without cause.' Then they told me they'd decided to outsource their psychiatric services instead of keeping them in house. But that doesn't make sense, because my colleague is still working there."

"Were there any problems between you and the medical group?"

"Not really. I mean, there were a lot of changes happening. They partnered with this new management group, First Choice. Those people hired this new pharmacology director, Jim Hirsch. He and I had a few disagreements, but that didn't affect my work with my patients."

Steve's mind-set was one I'd seen many times before with my physician clients. He was a dedicated healer who just wanted to treat his patients as best he could. He seemed almost naïve about the types of financial motives that can affect treatment policies and personnel decisions at health-care organizations.

"Tell me about this Hirsch person."

Steve explained the memos that had gone out and how he had ignored them because he didn't think the new prescription policy was in his patients' best interest. He didn't seem to fully grasp the connection between the memos and his termination. But I'd seen this pattern many times before. Steve had been fired for not playing ball, plain and simple. Whether anything illegal had taken place remained to be seen.

"Listen, Dr. Han, I think you may be too close to this to see the full picture. Why don't you bring me all your records and let me see what I can find?"

He still seemed reluctant to make trouble and uncertain as to whether he had any sort of case. After he left, I didn't hear from him for a while.

When Steve returned to my office a few weeks later, he came bearing records. Boxes of them. "I'm still not sure about this," he said, plunking down the heavy load, "but I've been giving it a lot of thought. My old patients are getting worse, my practice is suffering, and I'm hearing through the grapevine that NPG—or First Choice, I'm not sure which—is still interfering with referrals to me. It isn't right."

"I'll take a look at your records and let you know what I think we have."

I took his boxes and shook his hand.

15

I'm a detail-oriented attorney. Sometimes to a fault. I like to look at every scrap of paper I can put my hands on, because I never know when I'm going to stumble across some seemingly minor detail that might hold the key to an entire case.

As I began to dig through Steve's papers—sitting on my outdoor patio, as I like to do—I could see a familiar pattern in the memos from Hirsch and the other medical directors at First Choice. The early ones were general in nature, aimed at all employees. Then they became more insistent and more specific to Steve, saying, in effect, "You *need* to switch your patients to the medications we have approved."

The timing and sequence of the memos confirmed what I already suspected: Steve had been fired in a retaliatory manner for refusing to toe the party line. This belief was confirmed when I reviewed the Requests for Authorization that Steve had submitted after his termination so that he could continue seeing some of his former NPG patients. First Choice had rejected *every single one*. The same held true with his appeals. He was clearly being punished, starved out by his former employers.

I wrote up my thoughts for Steve, detailing the legal claims I believed we could make. Seeing those claims spelled out in black and white hardened Steve's resolve. He called me and gave me the thumbs-up to pursue the lawsuit.

The game was afoot.

I drafted a formal complaint and filed it in district court. When I file, I like to sue for several things—for example, wrongful termination, retaliation (which is illegal in California and some other states), interference with the doctor's ability to practice medicine, breach of contract, defamation, and/or other issues. The way I explain it to my clients is that I have to put all my ducks in a row, knowing that some of the claims might well be knocked down. I need at least one or two solid claims that will stand up throughout litigation.

I don't generally sue medical groups. Those are typically owned by doctors, who are the "worker bees" in the system. It's the management groups—or health-care systems—and the insurance companies behind them that I'm typically more interested in. They're the ones who make the big bucks, and they're the ones who create the money-driven policies that doctors are forced to follow. I suspected that most of NPG's "bad behavior" had really been ordered by First Choice, the management company. So it was First Choice I decided to sue.

First Choice, as expected, hired a huge law firm. The first thing their attorneys did—also as expected—was to file papers to try to have the case dismissed. This is standard practice in a lawsuit. They tried to claim I didn't have enough evidence, that my case wasn't strong enough, and so on. Again, standard stuff; I would have done the same if I were on the defense side. They also offered another interesting argument for dismissing the case: Dr. Han, they claimed, was actually doing *better* financially after opening his own practice than he had when he'd worked at NPG. Therefore, he hadn't suffered any damages.

Damages are a critical aspect of a suit. You need to show financial damages. If you can do that, you open the door for the jury to consider things like emotional damages and punitive damages as well, but if you can't show financial damage, the case won't make it into a courtroom.

I used the costs Dr. Han had incurred to start his new practice as the basis for our damages. It was a relatively small amount, but enough to get our foot in the door.

At our first hearing, the judge did dismiss one of our claims—one related to breach of contract, which I thought was our weakest—but he allowed the suit go forward on the other claims.

We were officially going to trial. Whew.

16

"Discovery," in case you're not familiar with the term, is a pretrial period in which both sides request evidence from the other side in order to "discover" what the opponents' case is built on. You can ask your opponent written questions, or *interrogatories*, such as "Why was my client terminated?" and "Who are the relevant witnesses?" You can also request that they produce documents.

In theory, the other side is supposed to comply with your requests in a complete and timely manner. Of course, we do not live in a theoretical world.

After submitting my discovery requests, I received nothing from the defense lawyers for weeks. I had to wait thirty days to receive any sort of response at all, and then I received nothing but a list of objections. Having worked for a large law firm, I knew this was par for the course. These firms have paralegals and associates whose sole job is to deliver discovery in the most confusing and least helpful manner possible. I had to file a motion with the court in order to make the defense send me the documents I had requested, and it was not until the eve of the hearing that I finally received them. But even then it was only a handful of docs. Not even close to what I'd asked for. So I had to file another motion and wait for the rescheduled hearing.

On the eve of *that* hearing, I finally received more documents. Boxes and boxes of them this time, which of course I had no time to go through. This is known as a "document dump." The opposition buries you in paperwork. There are rules against this, but all lawyers know how busy the courts are, and they know exactly what they can get away with. So they twist and bend the rules.

The document dump was meant to stymie me, and it had its desired effect. But it also made me excited. There must be something they're trying to hide, I reasoned, or they wouldn't be trying to bury it. My axiom is *the more grief they put you through, the more likely it is you're onto something.* There's a certain kind of excitement in looking for the needle in the haystack that they hope you will miss because it's so deeply buried.

I filed some more motions to show the judge that First Choice was deliberately hiding things from us, and he eventually appointed a "discovery referee." Even with the referee in place, First Choice continued to resist our requests for answers, documents, and depositions. This went on for the better part of the year, which only served to strengthen my conviction that the defense was hiding something critical.

When I finally had all the documents I needed, I began to see a pattern at play within First Choice—one that was much bigger than the termination of one doctor.

17

A name that appeared over and over in the docs was Dr. Jim Hirsch, a man Steve Han had mentioned several times. His official title was Director of Pharmacy and Formulary Administration. One of the first things I learned about him was that he was not actually a medical doctor. He had a PhD in pharmacology, but he had never been to medical school or treated a patient.

Yet when I sat down with him at the defense attorneys' offices to take his recorded deposition, he insisted upon being addressed as *Dr.* Hirsch. That gave me some insight into the man. One thing I've learned in my work is that there are a lot of educated people at the management level of insurance companies and health-care systems who have worked their way up the internal ladder but receive little recognition from the outside world. When you begin to grill them on their knowledge, they are often unable to resist the urge to show off a bit.

I could sense, as I was deposing "Dr." Hirsch, that he was eager to put me in my intellectual place after I'd pointed out to him that he wasn't a medical doctor. I hoped I could use his bruised ego to my advantage by playing dumb.

"You mentioned something a minute ago about 'the money First Choice saved on pharmacy costs,'" I said to him. "I'm confused about that, Mr. Hirsch."

"*Doctor* Hirsch."

"How can First Choice save money on pharmacy costs when it doesn't own or run a pharmacy? Can you explain that to me?"

"That's because of a practice in the health-care industry known as *risk sharing*." He said this with the air of a professor schooling an undergraduate.

"'Risk sharing,' did you say? Can you explain that to me?" I knew what risk sharing was, but I wanted to hear him explain it.

Hirsch sighed imperially. "It's an arrangement that a health-care provider, such as First Choice, makes with an insurance company. The provider is assigned a . . . *pool* of patients and agrees to provide *all* of the health-care services for those patients. In exchange, the provider is paid what's called a 'capitated fee.'"

"Which is?"

"Essentially a flat fee, per month, per patient."

"Hmm, 'flat fee.' So this amount doesn't go up or down, regardless of how much or how little treatment the patient receives?"

"That is correct."

"So . . . just to be sure I'm understanding this . . . if the actual cost of treatment First Choice provides for a patient comes in below the capitated fee, First Choice makes a profit on that patient; if the cost comes in higher, First Choice loses money. Is that right?"

"We prefer not to use terms like 'profit' and 'loss' when it comes to patient care, but, yes, essentially that's correct."

"So the less service First Choice provides, the more money it makes."

Hirsch didn't respond to that. Fine. The answer was self-evident.

I continued. "What happens in a situation where none of First Choice's physicians are able to provide the services a patient needs?"

"The patient is referred out of network."

"And how is that paid for?" I asked.

"That also comes out of the patient's capitated fee," he replied.

"So First Choice has to actually write a check to that outside physician?"

"The industry term for this is *leakage*." He was strutting his stuff now.

"I assume leakage is something management companies, such as First Choice, prefer to avoid?"

"Naturally."

It was clear now why First Choice kept refusing to approve Dr. Han's requests to see Karina and other of his former NPG patients out of network. First Choice would have had to foot the bill.

"And so how does this whole risk-sharing thing relate to pharmacy costs, Mr. Hirsch?"

"It's *Doctor* Hirsch, please," he replied testily. Then he said, "The costs of a patient's prescription medications come out of the capitated fee as well."

"Ah. So the more expensive a patient's medications, the less of the capitated fee First Choice gets to keep? That means it's in First Choice's direct financial interest to keep pharmacy costs as a whole down."

"We're not a charity organization, Ms. Barta. We have stakeholders. Before I came aboard, the company had to pay back nearly a million dollars to insurance companies due to patient-cost overages. That's not good business."

"So your cost-savings program was designed to save First Choice money by requiring physicians to prescribe lower-cost medications?"

"The program was voluntary," said Hirsch. "At least at first. But then certain physicians refused to cooperate."

"Physicians such as . . . ?"

"Dr. Han was one of them."

"How many others were there?"

"I'd have to look at my records."

"Dr. Han was the only one who continued to prescribe 'nonpreferred' medications to his patients, isn't that right, Mr. Hirsch?"

"That is probably correct."

"And he was the only doctor who was fired, isn't that also correct?"

"I'm not in charge of human resources."

"And how are *you* paid, *Mister* Hirsch?"

Hirsch raised his eyebrow at this question. I cast a glance at his attorney, expecting him to jump in, but for some reason, he remained mum.

"I'm paid in US dollars, *Miz* Barta," Hirsch replied in a caustic tone, his face flaring red. Then he calmed himself and said, "I receive a salary . . . plus bonuses."

"And what are those bonuses based on?"

"A number of performance measures."

"Isn't it true, Mister Hirsch, that you are paid a financial incentive based on the amount of money First Choice saves on pharmacy costs?"

Hirsch stared at me with open contempt, refusing to answer the question.

Finally, Hirsch's attorney spoke up and said, "I think we're finished here." Fine. Hirsch's nonanswer spoke volumes.

18

As the famous line goes: "Follow the money."

I sensed that the key to this case lay in finding out who, besides Hirsch, was profiting from the savings First Choice was netting on its reduced pharmacy costs. As I continued my discovery process, I learned that none of the treating physicians at NPG—i.e., the ones who actually saw patients—received bonuses or incentives of any kind. They were all paid straight salaries. Surprisingly low ones, too.

A lot of people assume doctors make a lot of money. Not necessarily so. People also assume that when doctors implement cost-savings measures for insurance companies, such as prescribing cheaper meds, they receive some kind of kickback. That's never the case. The people who make the money in these arrangements are the management, executives, and boards of directors. Some of these people *might* be doctors, but they're not the "treating patients" type of doctors. They're the "serve on boards and advisory panels" type.

As I dug further into First Choice's documents and kept asking questions, it became clear to me that the people who were reaping the rewards of First Choice's increased pharmacy profits were the members of the board.

I thought that might play in our case's favor. If I could paint a picture of a bunch of men in suits making money at the expense of both their patients and their hardworking physicians, I hoped a jury would eat it up and that it would make the reasons for Steve's firing seem obvious to them: he was costing the board money, and the board didn't like it.

When I started digging for information about the board, I must have touched a nerve, because suddenly First Choice began firing back. Steve informed me that he had been "served." NPG and First Choice had filed a cross-complaint against him, alleging that he had breached his employment contract when he worked there by seeing his own patients on the side. Even though these were indigent patients whom Steve had been seeing on a *pro bono* basis—and even though NPG knew about this arrangement and happily reaped the benefits from the good PR it gave them—they were now suing him over this.

Damn, this was hardball. Next, the defense team subpoenaed everyone who knew Steve professionally so that the whole medical community would know he was involved in a lawsuit, which the defense knew would look bad for him. First Choice also started changing its story about Steve's dismissal. They were no longer saying that he was terminated "without cause." They were now claiming there *had* been cause. But as I began to depose more witnesses within the company, I heard conflicting stories about what this cause was.

One witness testified, "We didn't renew his contract because we decided to outsource our psychiatric services." Hmm—then why did NPG keep another psychiatrist, Dr. Peters, on staff after Steve left?

Another witness stated that Steve was fired because he was "not financially beneficial" to the company. "He wasn't seeing enough patients." But I learned that Peters, the other staff psychiatrist, saw only half the number of patients Steve had seen.

Yet another witness testified to an exact opposite scenario, saying, "Dr. Han was *too busy* . . . and the more patients he saw, the more money the company lost."

This mishmash of conflicting stories had been told under sworn testimony. I hoped I could use that to make the defense look bad at trial. Which meant it would look very good for us.

19

I wasn't expecting a "smoking gun" in this case, but I got something close to it, and it came out of the blue.

We were near the trial date, and I finally had all the documents and information I needed from First Choice. I was working hard to organize it all, trying to stitch it together into a simple "story" that a jury would understand.

One Monday afternoon, I came into my office after a hearing, and my secretary told me a woman had called a couple of times asking for me. She said this woman had "something important" to tell me related to a case I was working on, but she'd refused to leave her name or say which case.

The next day, the same woman called again, but unfortunately I was on the phone at the time. My secretary asked her to hold, but she hung up. It seemed to my secretary that this woman was afraid of something.

By the end of the week, the woman hadn't called back. I was concerned. What did she know? Which case was it about? Why hadn't she called back?

That Saturday, I was in the office, preparing for the trial, when the phone rang. I grabbed it fast, before it went to voicemail.

A woman's voice spoke hesitantly. "Is . . . is Attorney Barta available?"

"This is Attorney Barta," I said.

"I . . . I don't quite know how to say this. I . . ."

"Is this the person who called before?" Silence. "Ma'am, I just want to assure you that our conversation will be absolutely confidential unless you tell me otherwise."

54

That seemed to relax her. "I work as a clerk for First Choice," she blurted out. "I answer the phone and process the Requests for Authorization we receive from doctors outside our network. I don't do the authorizing, just the processing. I . . . I don't know how to say this, but . . . I feel really terrible about what First Choice is doing to Dr. Han's patients."

I listened in silence as she marshaled the will to continue.

"Well . . . it all started one day when my supervisor came into the office and saw a pile of requests on my desk from Dr. Han. She picked them up, walked over to the shredder, and said—to the whole office, not just to me—'From now on, this is where all requests from Dr. Han will go.' Then she shredded the requests and told us all, 'You are not to give his phone number or address to anyone.'"

The caller went silent. I still didn't prod her. I've found that sometimes the best way to encourage people to talk is to say nothing at all.

"This has been going on for a long time," she said, "and I know it isn't right. One day, a young woman called me at the office—oh God, Attorney Barta!—she actually *pleaded* with me for ten minutes, telling me how important it was for her to see Dr. Han. And I felt terrible, just terrible, for her. I just can't do this anymore."

The mystery caller gave me permission to tell Dr. Han what she had told me. She also gave me her home phone and contact information.

She called me the following week and said she had spoken to other clerks in the department. They also felt bad about what they had been asked to do and were supportive of her coming forward. I told her that I would like to call her as a witness at trial, as well as the other clerks, and that if I subpoenaed them, they would be obligated to come to trial and tell the truth.

"I'm relieved, frankly," she said. "I want the truth to come out."

So did I.

I was growing eager to take this thing to trial.

PART III

A Psychiatrist's Tale

The Trial

20

"Bailiff, please send in the jury panel."

It's showtime.

I watch the prospective jurors as they file into the courtroom. Their faces betray the usual combination of curiosity, dread, and nervousness. One thing I can tell from watching their eyes is that many of them are thinking, "Wow, *this* is our courtroom? I thought it would be bigger."

Most people are surprised to learn that real courtrooms are much smaller and more cramped than the ones you see on TV. There's no room for slow, dramatic walks to the witness stand; everyone is on top of one another the whole time. The feel is more classroom than lecture hall.

We have a big jury panel today, close to a hundred men and women. For now, they all sit in the "gallery" section of the courtroom—that's the area beyond the "bar" that separates the court professionals from the audience.

I know that first impressions count, and the defense knows it too. I look over at the defense table. As always, it's swarming with pricey suits. We're suing a large, well-funded management company, and its defense team consists of two trial attorneys as well as the company's in-house attorney. (In-house lawyers don't usually speak at trial but rather serve as the "faces" of the defendants.) There's also a "trial tech" and a couple of other stray lawyers whose roles may be nothing more than to look important. Defense teams in these cases invariably try to put on a show of power. They want to convey the impression that they're the eight-hundred-pound gorilla that can't be taken down.

Fine, I say. Let them play Goliath. I prefer playing David. The plaintiff's table, by design, consists only of me, in my simple, formal skirt and heels (no power suits for me); my fashion-challenged doctor client, Steve Han; and a skinny, twenty-three-year-old trial tech who'll help me with the computer visuals.

That's it. If I ever have a need to use any other attorneys during the course of the trial, I'll have them sit in the gallery, and I won't interact with them in front of the jury. We're the little guy, and I want the jury to remember that.

Judge Javitz is a tall, imposing man with bushy eyebrows who looks every inch the part. The first thing he does is instruct the court clerk to seat a tentative jury in the jury box. The seats in the jury box are numbered, and the clerk calls out random names to fill each seat. Twelve jurors are chosen, plus two alternates. The clerk then calls six more names. They're known as the "six pack"; they'll wait on hand to fill jury seats as some of the seated jurors are dismissed.

The judge whips his glasses off—the glasses he'll use as a prop to intimidate the lawyers throughout the trial—and addresses the whole group of jury prospects, including those still seated in the gallery.

"Ladies and gentlemen, we are about to begin jury selection. Before we do, I want to explain a few things. First of all, terms. The 'plaintiff' is the party that brings the lawsuit; the 'defendant' is the party that defends against the suit. In this case, the plaintiff—the doctor sitting over there at the counsel table—used to work for the defendant, First Choice, a health-care management company. The plaintiff is suing the defendant for wrongful termination and retaliation." *As I listen to the speech I've heard so many times, I'm feeling confident in my case and hopeful in my mood, but I hasten to remind myself: you never know what's going to happen in a jury trial.* Judge Javitz then goes on to introduce all of the defense attorneys. It's a long list, and I'm afraid the jurors' heads are already spinning. "The main faces you'll want to remember, though, are Mr. Kurt Williams, who will be serving as the lead attorney for the defense, and Ms. Theresa Barta, the plaintiff's attorney."

After his statement, the judge reads off a list of witnesses who will be called in the trial and asks if any of the potential jurors know any of them or any of the attorneys. No hands go up, so the jury panel is handed over to me to begin voir dire—that's the process of asking questions in order to select an actual jury.

"They're all yours, counsel."

21

"I hate this part," I say as I step in front of the sea of expectant faces.

It might seem odd to open this way, but I do it for a couple of reasons. First, because it's true. I really do hate jury selection. Second, because I want to establish an honest relationship with the jury. One thing I've learned through years of trial work is that juries don't necessarily side with the person they *like* the most, but rather with the person they believe is telling the truth. And that begins with my being open and honest with them from moment one. Over the years, I've noticed that a lot of defense attorneys like to puff and posture for juries. I do the opposite. I act like myself because I believe that kind of honesty carries weight with a jury.

"I hate this part," I repeat, "because I have to go first, and I wish I didn't." Some of the jurors chuckle at this; others remain guarded. "I also hate it because I'm nervous, even though I do this for a living. But I know you're all nervous, too. So let's all just be nervous together." Some of the jurors seem to relax a bit when I say this; others continue to eyeball me stoically.

"But the main reason I hate jury selection is that I have to ask you some personal questions you might not want to answer. It might be uncomfortable for you. Well, I want you to know it's uncomfortable for me, too. But I have to do this, because the law calls for us to have fair jurors.

"Before I get into questioning those of you sitting in the jury box, I have a few questions I want to ask all of you, as a group."

Here I make sure to address everyone in the gallery as well; any of these folks could still end up on the jury. "How many of you have never seen a TV show or movie with a scene that takes place in a courtroom?" No hands go up. "Great. So you've all seen how a perfect trial looks, one with a carefully written script and trained actors. Well, there are no scripts in here. And I'm not perfect. I'm telling you right now, I'm *not* going to look like a TV lawyer, so please don't hold that against my client, OK?"

Next, I ask them all, "Has any of you ever had a doctor you didn't like?" This time, almost all hands go up. "Can anybody tell me a reason you don't like doctors?" This might seem like a risky strategy—soliciting anti-doctor talk when my client is a doctor—but I want to try to turn their attitudes around a bit before the trial even starts.

One woman says, "Seems like the only thing they care about anymore is the money. They don't spend any time with you."

"I hate that," I agree. "But did you ever stop to consider that maybe this isn't the doctor's fault? Maybe doctors would love to spend more time with you, but they're being pressured by their bosses to double-book and triple-book appointments so that the *clinic*, not the doctors, can make more money?"

The defense objects to this. Fine. I can see that some of potential jurors are already giving thought to what I said. And the early objection makes the defense team seem as if they're already worried about where this trial is headed.

Finally, I ask the whole group, "Does anyone have any issues with punitive damages being awarded in a lawsuit?" No one raises a hand, but I can see some furrowed brows and wary eyes. "I ask because I know a lot of you are looking at me suspiciously and thinking, 'She's one of those *plaintiff's lawyers* . . . one of those *greedy* plaintiff's lawyers. They're just in it for the money.' And I think some of you may believe that punitive damages are just a way for us greedy lawyers to make a lot of money.

"Let me explain something about punitive damages," I go on. "This is a civil case, not a criminal case. If it turns out the defendant did something wrong, no one is going to jail. Money is the only way to punish corporations for bad behavior. It's the only language they understand, and it's the only way to prevent them from repeating bad deeds. Would any of you have trouble awarding punitive damages?" No hands go up.

Now it's time to go through the lengthy process of questioning individual jurors. One of the main things I try to find out, besides the jurors' own backgrounds and experiences, is to whom they'll be talking when they go home at night. (Even though they're not "supposed" to talk to anyone about the trial, I know that many of them will.) So I ask questions about their significant others, their siblings, their adult children. If they have any family members who are doctors, lawyers, or insurance people, that can alter my enthusiasm about having them on the jury. My main purpose in voir dire, though, is to engage with the jury and start building a relationship with them.

Once I feel I've done my job in that regard, it's the defense's turn.

22

You might think that the person I'd be most familiar with at the start of a trial would be the opposing attorney. After all, both sides have been through a lengthy pretrial and discovery period. But the truth is, I don't usually meet my trial opponent until the day trial starts. That's because the pretrial stuff is typically handled by "lower level" attorneys. When trial day comes, though, the law firm puts forward one of its most senior litigators, usually one with decades of trial experience. These seasoned trial specialists typically have twenty years on me, both in terms of age and how long they've been practicing law.

Kurt Williams, the lead defense attorney, fits the bill. He comes off as quite the gentleman, polite, polished, unflappable—but also, in my opinion, a *bit* of a highbrow. I'm not sure how that approach is going to play with the jury.

"My name is Mr. Williams," he says addressing the large crowd of potential jurors. "The first thing I want you to know is that this is *not* a popularity contest. It should not matter if you like Ms. Barta more than me *or* whether you like her client more than mine." Odd way to start. It's as if he's acknowledging from the get-go that the defendant isn't very likeable. "You need to remain fair and objective." Then he singles out one juror and says, "Juror number six, can you do that? Can you be fair?"

Juror number six stammers, "Yes, I think so."

In my opinion, it's a mistake and a waste of time to ask jurors general questions like, "Can you be fair?" or "Can you be open minded?" The automatic answer to these questions is yes. Everyone *thinks* they can be fair. So a yes really tells you nothing. And on rare occasions when a juror answers no, the judge is likely to view that as a cheap attempt to wangle out of jury duty and will probably admonish that person, "Well, you're going to *have* to be fair."

I prefer to ask specific questions that address jurors' real biases about things that matter in the specific case at hand.

Williams makes another curious move a few minutes later when he says, "Juror number two, my partner over at counsel table, Mr. Singer, says that you seem familiar to him. Mr. Singer went to Yale. Do you recognize him?" He's clearly dropping the Yale reference to impress the crowd. But it backfires. Juror number two says, "No, not at all. And I didn't go to Yale. I couldn't have afforded that. I went to a junior college." Laughter in the courtroom.

Probably not the wisest idea to position your defense team as superior, in any way, to the jurors. Williams decides not to risk any more potential damage with the jury pool, and we move on to the challenge procedure.

There are two kinds of juror challenges that can be raised: *challenges for cause* and *peremptory challenges*. A challenge for cause comes up when a potential juror reveals something in his or her background or circumstances that is disqualifying, such as knowing one of the parties involved in the suit. When that occurs, either attorney can ask the judge to eliminate that juror, or the judge can do so on his/her own. Peremptory challenges, on the other hand, don't need to have a reason. Each side has a certain number of peremptory challenges they can use.

I don't like to use my peremptory challenges. Why? I feel it signals to the jury that I have something to worry about. I would rather project the sense that I am so confident about my case that it doesn't really matter who's sitting in the jury box.

So when the judge asks me if I'd like to use any of my challenges, I say, "No, your honor, I'm happy with the jury as it sits." I do this strategically, but as with any strategy, there's risk involved. You see, if the defense passes, too, the jury will become official right then and there. No challenges will be used at all. And the fact is, there are a couple of jurors I'm not too crazy about. My fingers are crossed right now.

But fortunately, Kurt Williams does use a couple of his challenges, to eliminate a young Hispanic male and a middle-aged Caucasian woman, so now my right to challenge kicks in again. I am able to eliminate the two jurors I was leery about.

After we finally seat a jury "in the box," the judge asks, one last time, "Is there any reason any of you feel you cannot serve?" A woman, surprisingly, raises her hand.

"I'm afraid I can't be on this jury, Your Honor," she says.

"And why's that, ma'am?" asks the judge.

"This is really embarrassing to say, but I don't think I'm smart enough. I don't understand contract language and medical terminology. I can't even understand my own medical bills or my health insurance policy."

The judge smiles at her kindly and says, "Thank you for your honesty, ma'am. But when it comes to contracts and medical language, I don't think any of us are very smart. I'm counting on Ms. Barta here to explain the issues so clearly that we all understand them." *Great, nothing like a little pressure.* "And if she doesn't explain things to your satisfaction, well, you don't have to vote her way."

Williams shoots me a little look that says, *Ha, you got yours too.* Touché.

So now we have our final jury seated. It's not an ideal one, but it rarely is. Probably the biggest issue in my mind is that three of the twelve jurors—as well as the judge—have received health-care bills from First Choice at one time or another. That can swing things either way. These jurors might be afraid to punish the company because they're afraid their health-care costs will go up. Or they might welcome the chance to "stick it" to a company they hate. You just never know. This is a risk I always run when suing large, familiar health-care organizations.

I look out at the jurors and try to get a feel for them as a group. A jury is a mysterious and precious thing. These twelve random men and women hold your client's fate—as well as decisions often worth tens of millions of dollars—in their hands. And they tend to be full of surprises.

One thing I do know about all juries, though, is that they don't want to feel their time is being wasted. They like to push through a trial as efficiently as possible. That's why I go into every trial with a keen awareness of a jury's "shelf life." In court, I rarely use objections or anything else that will slow a trial down. I even absorb tactical blows in the interest of speed and efficiency. I'm always trying to let the jury know that I respect their time.

That strategy has worked in the past. We'll see if it does this time.

The judge swears the new jury in. It's time for opening statements.

23

The plaintiff's table is always positioned closest to the jury. I like to sit in the actual chair that's nearest the jury, which means that, in most courtrooms, I'm close enough to the jury that I can literally touch one or two of them. I like to be close to the jury for one simple, primitive reason: physical closeness promotes personal closeness. But also, I know that the jurors are going to be looking at me all through the trial—do I flinch or take notes when something unexpected happens?—and I want them to know I'm at ease under scrutiny. That I have nothing to hide. I don't even take notes during trial, because I believe note taking signals concern (and besides, the jury is so close to me they could probably read any notes I'd take). From the opening gavel, I am subtly trying to establish a relationship of relaxed trust and familiarity with the jury.

That's why, when it's time for opening statements, I like to stand directly in front of the jury. If there's a podium set up—which there is, in this case—I move it out of my way. It's a symbolic gesture: there's nothing standing between you and me.

"Ladies and gentlemen of the jury," I say, launching into my opener—I go first because I'm on the plaintiff side. "The case you're about to hear is about money. My client is a doctor who was employed by the defendant. The evidence will show that the defendant, in the interest of making money, terminated my client in a retaliatory manner."

"Objection."

"Sustained."

I figured Williams would chime in. My opening statement is supposed to be a statement of the evidence I'm going to present, not an argument for a particular point of view. But as a plaintiff's attorney, I have to push the envelope a bit. I need to give the jury a taste for the story I'm going to tell.

"The way trials work," I continue to the jury, "is that we lawyers ask questions of a series of witnesses who swear to tell the truth. I go first because I'm the plaintiff's attorney. The defense goes next, and then I go again." Notice the plain, simple language I use. "I have the burden of proof," I say. "That means I'm the one who needs to persuade you that my client was wronged. But because this is a civil case, the burden of proof is not as high as in a criminal case. In a criminal case, you need to be convinced *beyond a reasonable doubt*. In this case, you only need to be convinced by the *preponderance of evidence*. That means 51 percent certainty is enough." Here I use hand gestures to show one hand just slightly outweighing the other. "I don't have to *absolutely* prove to you that things happened the way I say; I only need to convince you that my version of events is more likely than theirs."

A couple of jurors look surprised to hear this.

"Now, in this trial, you'll be shown evidence in a number of ways. Documents, testimony, photographs. They're the puzzle pieces. But they won't necessarily fall in logical order. The only way you'll be able to make sense of them is if you know what the whole picture is supposed to look like, kind of like a jigsaw puzzle. So I'm going to walk through the whole story with you, very quickly, so you'll know if something fits or doesn't."

I give them my quick synopsis of the case, trying to keep my focus on what the evidence will show.

"Now, I'd like to end with something I borrowed from the very first case I ever tried—something that always stuck with me. The opposing attorney told the jury, 'The easiest way to arrive at the truth is to remember this: facts don't lie, but people do.'" I pause to let the jury digest this. "Facts don't lie, but people do. The attorneys on both sides of this case are going to try to convince you of their point of view. Both sides have an agenda, myself included. But when it's time to decide what's true and what isn't, rely on the facts. E-mails, meeting notes, events, documents—things that haven't been created for your benefit or slanted for you but just are what they are. Those are the facts, and the facts don't lie. Thank you."

The defense's style couldn't be more different from mine. Kurt Williams carefully repositions the podium I moved aside and stations himself behind it—placing a large wooden object between himself and the jury. He's comfortable with formality, and it works for him. The first words out of his mouth are, "Let me tell you what this case is *not* about. This is not about money. Nor is it about a doctor who was wrongfully terminated. Evidence will show that the plaintiff was not, in fact, *terminated* by the defendant. This doctor's contract was simply not renewed. The defendant's written agreement with its doctors clearly states that it has a right not to renew contracts. It doesn't need a reason. Why not? Because businesses have a right to choose whom to do business with. Would you like to be told that you were *required* to shop at Safeway instead of Trader Joe's?" A couple of jurors shake their heads. "Of course not. Businesses have that same right. And when the defendant chose not to renew the plaintiff's contract, it was simply exercising a right of commerce. Money had nothing to do with it. But when this nonrenewal occurred, the doctor here was hurt and angry—and made a decision to go after the defendant for money. So, yes, this case *is* about money. But not in the way Attorney Barta suggests. It's about a doctor with wounded pride trying to seek revenge on a former employer."

At this point, I can feel the eyes of the jury boring in on Steve Han and me. *Stay calm,* I tell myself. *Don't react.* I have to trust that, over the course of the trial, I will be able to show the jurors that the defense's characterization of my client is way off base.

Patience, Theresa.

A trial teaches nothing if not patience.

Time to bring on the witnesses.

24

I like to put my client on the stand as my first witness. I want the jury to meet them, get to know them, and hear their story. I also want to signal that our side has nothing to hide or fear. It's important that the jury start to like and trust my client immediately.

After the swearing in and establishing of my client's name and credentials, I ask my client, "Have you ever been on the witness stand, Dr. Han?"

"No," replies Steve, looking intently at me.

I subtly swing my eyes toward the jury box, reminding my client to talk to the jury, not to me. We've gone over this in preparation for trial, but it's easy to forget it in the heat of battle. "Are you nervous today?"

"Scared to death is more like it," Steve says, turning uncomfortably toward the jury. "I think I'd rather be on the operating table right now."

A few of the jurors laugh. "Then why are you here," I ask, "if it's so painful to you?"

"Because I strongly believe I was wronged. More than that, I believe my patients were wronged—and are still being wronged—by the defendant's behavior."

"May I ask a few questions about you and your background?" I ask.

"If you must," my client says jokingly.

Again there are chuckles from the jury. They seem to like my client's unassuming shyness.

At this point, I do what I typically do: ask a bunch of questions about how he became a doctor, what his specialty is, how long it took him to earn his license and board certifications. I want the jury to see exactly how much time, effort, and money a doctor invests in becoming a working specialist.

Then I get into the more personal stuff.

"Do you like being a physician?"

"I love it. I love practicing medicine, psychiatry in particular. I've been called to this profession ever since I was in high school, and I've never wanted to be anything else."

"So why *are* you a doctor—you, personally?"

"It's all about the patients for me. I get a tremendous sense of satisfaction helping patients overcome mental-health challenges and live fuller lives—although, these days, there's a lot of pressure on doctors to spend less time with their patients."

"You must make a lot of money doing what you do."

"Not as much as people think. And after I pay my malpractice insurance, I make a *lot* less." A couple of jurors laugh. "Becoming a doctor was never about money to me."

Just FYI, I can only ask open-ended questions of this witness. The only time lawyers are allowed to ask "leading questions" is when a witness has been designated as hostile. Then we can ask questions like, "Isn't it true that you hated your neighbor and wanted her to die?" Otherwise, we're not allowed to troll for a particular answer.

"Do you think you're a good doctor?" I ask.

"I believe I am. I've had the highest patient satisfaction ratings of any doctor at the medical group, irrespective of specialty. I've never had any complaints about my patient care. Lots of doctors refer their patients to me. If I weren't a good doctor, they wouldn't do that. But most of all, my patients often tell me they love me. And I love them. They're like family to me. In fact, that's what probably got me in trouble with the defendant."

"What do you mean?"

"Well, I was always putting my patients first, which meant I sometimes had to fight for them to receive the best treatment. I saw this as my ethical responsibility, even if it rubbed some people the wrong way."

"And how did you do that—fight for your patients?"

"When policies were created that were not good for patient care, I spoke up against them. Most of these revolved around prescription medications. I prescribed the medications I believed were best for my patient, not just those on the list of preapproved medications that management pressured us to prescribe."

"Why did you go against your employer's recommendations regarding medications?"

"Psychiatric medications are not all alike. Patients often respond very well to one medicine while not responding at all—or perhaps even having negative reactions—to a very similar one. Even generics of the same medication that are made by different companies have varying levels of effectiveness for different patients. It's not a one-size-fits-all situation, where you can give the same medicine to every patient who has the same diagnosis—though that was what First Choice was essentially telling us to do."

"Your decision to prescribe according to your own medical judgment—did that behavior become an issue for you, in terms of your relationship with the defendant?"

"It did. I began to receive memos from First Choice's administrative staff—one person in particular—informing me that my practices were not in line with the company's policies."

"And at some point, were you terminated?"

"Yes."

"What was the reason you were given for your termination?"

"No reason."

"It just happened out of the blue?"

"Pretty much."

I look at the jury; they're alert and attentive. "Now I'd like to talk about the effect this termination has had on your life. Beyond the loss of a salary—which in itself I'm sure was devastating—can you tell us how this has affected your life?"

"It's been hard. Your self-esteem takes a blow. I worked twelve years to become a board-certified psychiatrist. I'd never been disciplined, never been accused of malpractice, never had any patient complaints. I couldn't figure out what I had done wrong." Here my client's voice actually cracks. "All I did was try to give my patients good, conscientious care, which I thought was my job as a physician and a mental-health professional."

"How did the termination affect your medical practice?"

Steve proceeds to explain the struggles he had starting his own private practice. He describes the financial difficulties, the stress, and the trouble he had reconnecting with his old patients, mainly because First Choice made it difficult for his patients to find him. He shares a few of the false stories his patients were told about why he left NPG. I can see some of the jurors frowning in disapproval about the clinic's behavior, so I decide this is a good time to end my questioning of Dr. Han.

"Thank you, doctor. No further questions."

"Mr. Williams, you may cross-examine the witness," says Judge Javitz.

25

In my pretrial conferences with my client, I repeatedly emphasized, "During cross-examination, you'll be on your own. Don't look at me. Especially if you're asked a tough question. You don't want to look like you're turning to your lawyer to bail you out. In fact, if you *do* turn to me, I'll be no help because *I* won't be looking at *you*." And it's true; I never look at my clients when they're being cross-examined; I keep my eyes down and occupied. "Just be honest and answer the questions truthfully," I told Steve. "You're on the right side of this, and the jury will see that."

What I don't tell my clients is that while they're being crossed, I will be quietly dying inside. The vast majority of the time, they do a great job. But inevitably, in every case, a couple of landmines turn up. There is no such thing as a perfect case.

Williams goes after my client in a few ways. His first tack is to ask about the salary my client was earning at the medical group and is earning now.

"Isn't it true that you're making more money now than you did when you worked for the medical group?"

Dr. Han hesitates, but then answers, "Yes, but it wasn't that way at first."

"Still, would it be fair to say that, economically speaking, you're better off now than you were two years ago?"

Steve is forced to admit this is true. The defense will use this admission to claim there were no damages to my client. That's OK. I knew this would come up.

Next Williams tries to paint my client as angry and vengeful.

"Can you describe your feelings toward your former employer after you were terminated? Were you angry?"

"I wasn't happy, that's for sure. Mainly, I was hurt and confused."

"You testified that you felt you were doing a good job, and then you were suddenly let go, with no explanation offered. Are you saying you weren't angry about this at all?"

I could protest where this is headed, but, again, I don't like to object. I've heard jurors say over and over again, "I don't understand why they keep objecting. Why don't they just present the case and let us make our decision?" To jurors, a trial full of objections is like watching a football game where there's a penalty flag on every play. So I keep my mouth shut.

"There was some anger, of course," replies my client.

"And do you expect the jury to believe that this anger had nothing whatsoever to do with your decision to file a lawsuit?"

"I can only tell the truth," answers my client. "My motivation in filing the suit was primarily one of conscience. I knew patients were being harmed."

Williams lifts his eyebrows at the jury as if to say, *Believe that crock if you want, but you and I know better.*

26

When deciding whom to call as my next witness after putting my client on the stand, I try to land a solid blow. In this case, I decide my best shot is with the pharmacy director, Dr. Hirsch.

Hirsch represents the prescription medication issue, which is at the heart of Steve's firing and a common theme in the cases I try. Very often, someone at the health-care system and/or insurance company starts pressuring doctors to use cheaper generic medications, and my client, as a doctor, disagrees with that policy. This becomes part of the reason for the termination (though the defendant usually denies this).

"The plaintiff calls James Hirsch."

Hirsch takes the stand and gives me a chilly smile. Based on our previous experience during depositions, I know he doesn't like me.

"What is your title at First Choice, Dr. Hirsch?"

"I am Director of Pharmacy and Formulary Administration," he says.

"And were you hired to run a program called the Drug Cost and Savings Plan?"

"I was."

"And what is the goal and purpose of that program?"

"To contain some of the costs associated with prescription medications."

"Contain costs for whom?" I ask.

"Well, for my employer, of course," replies Hirsch.

"Then would you agree that, by definition, in order to do your job well, you need to be effective in reducing the amount of money First Choice spends on patients' medications?"

"I prefer the term 'containing costs' to 'reducing spending.'"

"I'm sure you do. But the program is really about saving money, isn't it?" Because Hirsch is a hostile witness, I am allowed to lead him somewhat with my questioning.

"There's a lot of waste in medicine," he replies.

I then get him to agree that Dr. Han was seen as an outlier because of a pattern of prescribing medicines that were not on First Choice's "preferred" list.

"Are you paid an incentive in addition to your salary, Dr. Hirsch?"

"I am."

"And what is that bonus based on?"

"I don't recall all of the details."

"Surely you recall some of them, though. Is your bonus, or is it not, based on the amount of money you save the company on drugs?" I remember that Hirsch refused to answer this question during his deposition, but now he'll be forced to answer it.

Attorney Williams jumps to his feet and says, "Objection. Irrelevant. How Dr. Hirsch's compensation is calculated has nothing to do with this case."

"No arguments, please, counsel," Judge Javitz admonishes him. "Just state your objection. If you want to argue your reasons, request a sidebar. Objection overruled."

So Hirsch is forced answer my question. "I'm not sure exactly how my incentive is calculated," he says.

He's evading the point, and I know it. I don't want him to get away with it.

"Regardless of how your bonus is *actually* calculated, in all of its fine details, is it your *understanding* that your bonus is tied, in a general way, to the amount of money you save the company on pharmacy costs?"

"Objection, Your Honor."

"Sustained, as phrased," says the judge. When a judge says, "As phrased," what he's really telling you is that if you ask the question a different way, he may allow it.

I give it one more try. I know I look like I'm asking faulty questions, but the jurors are hearing the defense team strenuously objecting to this line of questioning, which is one of my goals. This time, I say, "The whole purpose of the program you run is to save money on pharmacy costs. It's *called* the Drug Cost and Savings Plan. Isn't it safe to say that the amount of money you save on pharmacy costs each year is a major factor in the amount of bonus you receive?"

"Objection, Your Honor," says Williams, "and I would like to request a sidebar."

The judge looks at the clock; he knows this will slow everything down. At this point, I think the answer I've been angling for is obvious to the jury: Hirsch is financially incentivized for saving the company money on medications. And my client's behavior was affecting his bonus money.

In order to show respect for the court's time and the jury's time (and win a few points for considerateness), I say, "Never mind, Your Honor. I'll withdraw the question. I think my point has been made."

27

I hope to get more from Hirsch. I remember from his deposition that he has quite an ego; perhaps I can use that in my favor.

I say to him, "There are a lot of doctors who work for the various medical groups under First Choice management, and many of them are highly trained specialists. Who is in charge of telling them what medications they should be using?"

"I am," he says, looking out at the jury and the audience, his ego aglow.

Good. Now I aim for his pressure point. "During your deposition, you were quite insistent that I call you 'doctor.' Why was that?"

"Because I *am* a doctor. I spent many years in school achieving that title, and it designates my expertise."

"You mention schooling, Dr. Hirsch. Can you please tell the jury what schooling you're referring to?"

"I have a bachelor of science degree, a masters, and a PhD. I also have a great many other training certifications, which I can happily show you."

"Thank you. And so where did you go to medical school?"

"My doctorate is a PhD," he says scornfully, as if *I'm* the one in need of schooling. "That is not the same as an MD. It is a different course of study entirely, though one that also represents a substantial amount of investment, effort, and academic achievement."

I'm letting him "lecture" me for a reason. I'm guessing the judge will soon tire of it and order him to restrict himself to simple answers. Then I'll make my strategic move: I'll start asking him more critical questions, and he won't be able to wriggle out of them with verbiage. That's my hope, anyway.

"It was a simple question, Mr.—ahem, *Doctor* Hirsch. You didn't go to medical school, did you?"

"No, I did not, but my education has nonetheless been—"

The judge chimes in, as I hoped he would. "Just answer Ms. Barta's questions with a yes or no, Doctor Hirsch. Please don't add anything. It just makes everything take longer, and we don't want to waste the jury's time."

I repeat my question, "You never went to medical school, did you?"

Hirsch stares daggers at me. "No."

"You are not a medical doctor, are you?"

"No, but—"

"Ah-ah," Judge Javitz interrupts the witness again. "Yes or no only, please."

Hirsch says, unhappily, "No."

"You've never treated a patient in your life, have you?"

"No." More daggers.

"And yet you're the one telling medical doctors, who *did* go to medical school and who *are* taking care of patients, what medications they should be prescribing?"

"Yes, I am." He says this, again, with a misplaced sense of pride that is not serving his cause.

"And you do that without ever meeting any of the patients, reviewing their medical records, or knowing anything about their specific needs, correct?"

"Yes." Less pride now, more annoyance.

"No more questions, Your Honor."

I look over at the jurors. I hope I have succeeded in conveying the impression—the true impression—that Hirsch's job is to save money for First Choice, that he is paid an incentive for convincing doctors to prescribe cheap generic medications (an effort my client resisted), and that he himself is not a medical doctor and has never treated a patient in his life. And yet here he is telling "real" doctors how to treat *their* patients. Who could blame my client, a skilled physician, for taking issue with such a scenario? That is the thought I hope I've left lingering in the jurors' minds.

28

Williams does a noble job of trying to rehabilitate Hirsch. He tries to paint him as a knowledgeable expert who merely served as a "resource" for doctors. Hirsch didn't *tell* doctors what to do; he only offered guidelines. One of the pieces of evidence Williams presents is a "formulary table" that Hirsch gave out to the doctors. It shows lists of "preferred"—not *required*—medications. This table turns out to be one of the big surprises in the trial.

Have I mentioned the fact that I'm a huge football fan? My brother worked for the Minnesota Vikings for over twenty years, and some of my old school friends have gone on to play professional football. I often compare a trial to a football game. A coach can make the best game plan ever, but still, it's the *un*planned events that happen on the field—a fumble, a missed tackle—and the way you react to them in real time that often wins or loses the game. Similarly, in a trial, you can meticulously plan every aspect of your trial strategy, but it's often the unexpected things—and how you react to them—that win or lose a case.

When the defense puts Hirsch's formulary table up on the screen, something looks off to me. I don't have a photographic memory, but something is bugging me about it. I go to one of my trial boxes and dig out my own copy of this document—the version that was *actually* given out to doctors. I can't believe what I'm seeing. The version on the screen has slightly different wording in some of the explanatory sentences. Instead of saying doctors "should" take certain steps, it says they "may wish" to do so. Instead of saying doctors are "expected" to follow the guidelines, it says they are "encouraged" to do so. The version on screen subtly supports the defense's claim that the drug program was more voluntary than it really was.

Someone has tried to pull a fast one here. This is huge.

I wait patiently for Williams's cross-examination to end, and then I come back on rebuttal. "I'll keep this short," I promise the jury, "but there's one thing I need to clear up." After establishing that my copy of the formulary table is the one that was actually given to my client when he worked for NPG, I ask to have it displayed next to the defense's version. I say to Hirsch, "Do these two documents look the same to you?"

"Yes," replies Hirsch. Give the man an A for effort.

"There's no difference between them?"

"Not that I can see."

"Look a little more closely, please. Look at the version number in the corner. Is the number the same on both versions?"

A pause. He knows he's in trouble. "No."

"Look at the third word in the second sentence. Is that the same in both documents?"

"No."

"Look at the fourth word in the fifth sentence. Is that the same in both documents?"

"No."

"The version you have presented in court is not the same version that was originally handed out to doctors, is it?"

"Apparently not."

"Well, who created the document you've been showing the jury today?"

"I did."

"And you created it just for this trial, didn't you?"

"Yes," he replied smugly.

Wow. Neither the judge, the jury, nor Kurt Williams can hide his surprise. Someone on the defense side has substituted a more favorable document for the actual one that had been handed out to Dr. Han and the other doctors at NPG.

Court is over for the day, but as I'm leaving, I hear the defense team in the hall, arguing heatedly. Williams seems genuinely upset that this switcheroo has happened. He knows how bad it makes the defense look.

We have just scored a fluke touchdown and then recovered the kickoff on a fumble. The game is far from over, but this is a biggie.

29

A big problem that can occur in trials is that witnesses disappear or fail to show up. I sometimes find out a week, a day, or even an hour before a key witness is supposed to testify that they're "in the wind." I have also had witnesses simply refuse to show up.

In this case, the former CEO of First Choice, Don Barker, actually tells me point blank on the phone that he has no intention of showing up in court, even though I have subpoenaed him. "I'm not coming, Ms. Barta, so deal with it."

I have to go to the judge and report this situation. Javitz is not happy. He tells the defense team, "You'd better have Mr. Barker here tomorrow morning, or I will issue a bench warrant and have him arrested."

Court is due to start at 9:00 a.m. the next day, and I subpoena Barker to show up at 9:30 just so he won't run into any jurors when he arrives.

Well, Barker takes it upon himself to show up an hour early, so when I come into the courthouse the next morning, whom do I find him gabbing in the hallway with? None other than the jurors themselves! This is a *major* no-no. I don't want to appear alarmed, so I say, politely but firmly, "Mr. Barker, will you come with me, please?" I march him right into the courtroom and tell him, as if he were an errant schoolkid, "Sit down there, shut your mouth, and don't move."

When I explain to the judge what happened, he is outraged. With the jury out of the room, he puts Barker on the stand and demands to know why he's been talking to the jurors.

"I didn't know they were jurors," claims Barker.

"So none of them were wearing their jury tags?" inquires the judge.

Barker can't weasel out of this one. The judge is livid. He summons the jury members into his chambers, one by one, and questions them about what Barker said to them. The consensus is that Barker was talking trash about me. Fine; I have thick skin. But here's the funny thing: he was doing it to such an extreme degree that the jurors actually think he's unbalanced.

So his little attempt at jury swaying has backfired, and now his credibility is in shambles. Seeing this, the defense team moves for a mistrial, but the judge tells them, "Oh, no. You should have controlled your own witness. Now you're going to have to live with the consequences."

And one of those consequences is that I'm now going to try to poke more holes in Barker's credibility.

I put him on the stand, and after establishing the basics—that Barker is the former CEO of First Choice and that my client worked for a medical group Barker was in charge of—I ask him, "Did the doctor, my client, leave while you were still with the company?"

"Yes."

"The doctor was terminated, correct?"

"No, it was a business decision not to renew the doctor's contract."

"A business decision," I say. "And what was the reason for that decision?"

"Strictly financial. We decided that we were going to contract with an outside group for our behavioral health services, which included psychiatrists."

"I see. And do you employ a Dr. Randall Peters on your staff at the NPG clinic?"

"Yes, we do."

"And can you tell us what Dr. Peters's specialty is?"

"He's a psychiatrist."

"I'm confused. You just testified that First Choice had decided to outsource its psychiatric services. So why is Dr. Peters, a psychiatrist, still employed on your in-house staff?"

"His contract was deemed to be financially advantageous to the company."

"Isn't the reason Dr. Peters was retained while Dr. Han was terminated because Dr. Peters stuck faithfully to the company's prescribing guidelines?"

"Dr. Han was terminated for reasons of contractual policy!"

Barker's facial expression says he realizes he has just made a huge mistake. He has admitted to terminating Dr. Han.

"But you just testified that the doctor was *not* terminated. So which is it?"

Barker replies, "My recollection and understanding was that the doctor's contract was simply not renewed. I misspoke just now in the context of your questioning."

"Was the decision to terminate—or 'not renew,' whatever we decide to call it—Dr. Han's decision or the defendants'?"

"It was a business decision."

"I see. This 'business' makes decisions all by itself?" The jury laughs. "*You* were involved in that decision, were you not, Mr. Barker?"

"Yes."

"And the decision was made by you, not the doctor, right?"

"Yes."

"In other words, it was not the doctor's choice to leave, right?"

"That's correct."

At this point, I introduce into evidence a letter exchange between a patient, Karina Meyers, and First Choice. It begins with a request by Karina to continue seeing Dr. Han as her doctor, out of network, after his termination occurred. The evidence shows that the patient's request was denied and that Karina followed this up by sending a letter directly to the CEO, Charles Barker.

"Would you read the first sentence of your reply letter to this patient?" I instruct Barker.

With a dismissive shake of his head, he reads, "As you know, your doctor chose to leave our medical group to return to private practice."

"You personally wrote this letter in response to the patient, isn't that right?"

"Yes."

"So it was not a form letter, correct?"

"It was not."

"So you made a conscious decision to tell this patient that her doctor had left the medical group voluntarily, did you not?"

"Apparently so."

"But that's not true, is it, Mr. Barker? That my client left voluntarily?"

"No."

"I have nothing more for this witness, Your Honor."

Sometimes, when a witness is caught in a lie, your best move is to leave them hanging on the lie, even if you have a few more questions you'd like to ask.

30

I have only two witnesses remaining, and they shouldn't take too long.

The next witness I call is the former patient of Dr. Han, Karina Meyers, who wrote the letter to Barker. After she is sworn in, Judge Javitz makes it clear that she does not need to disclose to the jury her medical condition or any treatments she received.

"At some point in the past," I ask Karina, "were you treated by the doctor, my client?"

"Yes, I was his patient for many years."

"Were you happy with the treatment you received?" I inquire.

"Yes, absolutely. I had a complicated condition, and Dr. Han was the only one who was ever able to help me manage it effectively."

"And, at some point, did you have to stop treating with Dr. Han?"

"Yes, I did," replies Karina.

"How did that come about? Can you tell the jury, please?"

"I went in for my regular appointment," says Karina. "When I went up to the desk, I was simply told I would be seeing a different doctor."

"Were you told why?"

"Not at first, but I kept pushing for an answer. I wanted to know where *my* doctor went. Finally, some management person told me that Dr. Han had left the medical group and started a private practice."

"What did you think when you heard that?"

"I was surprised. Shocked, actually. I couldn't believe Dr. Han would just abandon me like that, without notice, after years of working together."

"Is that how you felt? Abandoned?"

"Absolutely. I had been . . . struggling with my illness . . . for a long time before seeing Dr. Han, and I was finally getting the treatment I needed. For my doctor to just up and leave me . . . made me feel unimportant, uncared for, abandoned, scared. It was horrible."

"Did ever find out what actually happened to the doctor?"

"Eventually, yes."

"How?"

"Well, I . . . got really . . . um, sick . . . and ended up in the hospital. Someone called Dr. Han to find out how to best treat me."

"After you left the hospital, did you try to continue seeing Dr. Han?"

"Yes, but I couldn't."

"Why not?"

"I was told that I needed a referral, and when I requested one, I was told that the referral was not approved."

"Did that affect your care in any way? Again, you do not need to disclose details about your treatment or condition."

"Yes. The new doctor I was assigned said I needed to be on different medicine. One that was cheaper and approved by First Choice. But the side effects were horrible, and it didn't work like the medication I had been on before. Also, I wasn't seen as often by the new doctor, and my visits were much shorter. It was obvious he didn't really care about me like Dr. Han, my real doctor, did. He just wanted to write me a generic prescription."

"Did you complain to anyone?" I ask her.

"Yes," she replies. "I asked the front office if it was possible to have someone reconsider my requests to see *my* doctor. And that's when they said they could not give me a referral because my doctor had been fired for providing treatment that was not medically necessary."

At this, I can almost hear the jury gasp.

31

"What did you think when you heard your doctor had been fired?"

"It didn't sound right to me, because Dr. Han had always given me great medical care. But then I started thinking that maybe I was the exception. Maybe there was some good reason he was fired. Maybe this doctor I thought I trusted was providing unnecessary services to make more money."

I look at Steve's eyes, and I see them well with tears.

"Did that make you think badly of Dr. Han?" I ask the witness.

"Yes, kinda."

"Is my client still your doctor today?"

"No."

"Would you like Dr. Han to still be taking care of you?"

"Absolutely, very much so."

"Can you explain why you're not treating with him anymore?"

"Because I can't get a referral," says Karina.

"How do you feel about that?"

"Really upset, actually," she says. And then, in a voice laden with sarcasm, she adds, "But it doesn't seem to matter what *I* think or want or feel. After all, I'm only the patient. What do *I* know about what's best for me?"

"I have no further questions. Thank you so much for coming in."

The younger attorney for the defense, Rachel Carnes, stands up. She is finally going to get her chance to "be a lawyer." She smiles, introduces herself to the witness, and says, "I have just one question for you, Ms. Meyers. You testified that the reason you're not treating with the plaintiff today is because you can't get a referral. Isn't the *real* reason you're not treating with the plaintiff the fact that the plaintiff is not contracted with your insurance company?"

What is she going for here? This question doesn't even make sense. If she wants to go down the insurance path, I'm happy to show that the reason *my client no longer takes Karina's insurance is because of the "blacklisting" that took place in the wake of my client's firing.*

I don't need to say a word, though, because Karina fires back with ferocity: "No! The reason I can no longer receive treatment from *my* doctor—whom you could at least call by name, instead of 'the plaintiff,' and whom I absolutely love, by the way—is BECAUSE YOUR CLIENT WON'T REFER ME!"

"No further questions, Your Honor," says Carnes, hurrying back to the safety of the defense table.

I have finally come to my last witness, Amy Rogers. She turns out to be a toughie. Not because she is hard to question, but because she pulls a runner. This is the woman who called me, very reluctantly, during discovery—I'm sure you'll recall her—to share a damaging story about being ordered to shred documents in her office. She finally agreed to testify, but then she got cold feet again, and I had to subpoena her.

Well, the day of her testimony, I have her waiting in a conference room down the hall from the courtroom. When court is about to start for its afternoon session, I go to retrieve her, and lo and behold, she has vanished!

I call her cell number in a panic, and she says, "I'm sorry, Ms. Barta, but I chickened out. I can't go through with it. When I saw my boss in the hallway outside the courtroom, I knew I couldn't stand up there and testify against her."

"Look, I am very grateful to you for coming forward as you did," I tell her, "but you can't back out now. You are under subpoena."

She is nearly in tears as she tells me that she doesn't know what to do. When I return to the courtroom, I ask for a sidebar so I can explain the situation to the judge. He agrees to recess for the day, to give me time to persuade this witness to come back the next morning. Thankfully, I am able to convince Ms. Rogers to come back, but only because I tell her that Dr. Han has offered her a job in the event she is fired.

Finally, Amy Rogers is on the witness stand, looking about as comfortable as a mackerel at a fish fry.

"Can you please tell the jury who your employer is, Ms. Rogers?" I ask her.

"The defendant, First Choice," she says, studying her nails as if the meaning of life were written on them.

"How long have you worked there?"

"Seven years."

"Have you agreed voluntarily to come in and testify today?" I say.

"Not really." Her body language accentuates her answer.

"Can you explain what you mean by that?"

"Well, I'm afraid I might get fired."

"Why is that?" I ask her.

"Because I know that I was supposed to keep this secret."

"And who told you that?"

"Well, they didn't actually use the word 'secret.' We were just told that we were not to talk about it, my coworkers and I."

"I see. And who was it that said that to you?"

"The medical director of the department I work in, Referrals and Authorizations." She shifts her eyes nervously toward an older woman sitting in the gallery and then quickly looks down at her nails again.

"Can you tell us what your department does, Ms. Rogers?"

"When patients want to receive certain types of medical services or to be referred to a particular doctor outside the network, we receive a 'Request for Referral.' My job is to fill out a form based on the information we receive and then forward everything to the medical director, who decides whether to authorize or deny the referral."

"Did you ever receive any 'Requests for Referrals' for patients to see my client, Dr. Han, after he was terminated?"

"Yes."

"How many?"

"I don't know the exact number, but lots!"

"And did you prepare the necessary forms for each Referral Request and provide them to your medical director?"

She casts a dark glance toward the older woman in the gallery and says, "No."

"Why not?" I ask her.

"Because . . . well, because one day, I had a stack of requests sitting on my desk—all for your client, Dr. Han—and the medical director walked in. When she saw Dr. Han's name on the stack, she grabbed the whole pile of requests, walked across the room, and put them into the shredder. She announced to everyone in the department, 'This is where all Requests for Referrals for Dr. Steven Han should go from now on.'"

"And did you follow the medical director's orders?"

"I had to. From that time on, I put all Requests for Referrals for the plaintiff into the shredder." The jury gasps audibly. "I didn't want to, and I felt really bad about doing it. But, like I said, I really need my job."

The look on the defense attorneys' faces speaks volumes. They don't even object. I think they are in shock. Even though this witness was on my witness list, they obviously had not talked to her. And now there is no way for her testimony to be undone.

Knowing when to quit is an essential aspect of being a trial attorney.

"The plaintiff rests, Your Honor."

32

Now it's time for the defense to present its case. As a rule, by the time we arrive at this part of the trial, I have to hope that I've already won. I have to hope the jury likes my client, believes in me, and is leaning heavily toward finding in favor of my client. Why? Because now it's the defense's turn to try to make my client look bad. And human nature is such that if we like someone, we tend to disregard the negative things we hear about that person, but if we dislike someone, we soak up the negative stuff like a sponge. Trials are no different.

The defendant, as sometimes happens in cases like this, has painted itself into a bit of a corner by insisting that Dr. Han was not terminated. That means the defense can't really embark on an all-out character assault—pointing out all the things Steve did wrong—because then it will seem as if he *was* terminated. So Williams calls a couple of human-resources witnesses to testify that Steve's contract permitted nonrenewal without cause. He also calls a VP who testifies that First Choice did, in fact, decide to outsource NPG's behavioral health services. (But, of course, the defense still has the problem that Dr. Peters, the other psychiatrist, remained on staff.) Finally, Williams calls one of First Choice's medical directors. And here is where they *do* try to make Steve look bad. The director testifies that Steve had a habit of ignoring internal memos and, in general, showing contempt for management. He points out a couple of minor areas, besides the drug policy, where Steve had disagreements with management. The purpose of this testimony is to counter my argument that Steve was fired because of his prescribing patterns. The picture the defense tries to paint, without overstating it, is that although Steve was a fine doctor, he was a pain in the butt to work with, and so, when it came time to renew his contract, First Choice simply exercised its right not to renew.

Now it's time to see whose version of the truth the jury believes.

The day of closing arguments has finally arrived. It all comes down to this. This is my big chance to pull all the pieces together and make an actual argument. Here is where I get to present my full narrative, complete and in order, told the way *I* want to tell it, in all of its Technicolor detail.

There's one problem, though. This trial has stretched on for weeks. The jury is tired and restless and just wants its chance to deliberate. So, as much as I want to present a lengthy argument that covers every point that's gone our way throughout the trial, I have to remind myself that the jury doesn't want to hear it all. My challenge is to squeeze my closing argument down to its bare essentials, so that I can present it to the jury quickly and cleanly and wrap up on a winning note. This means reducing pages and pages of arguments to a half page of bullet points.

I've worked hard on my closing. For three days, I have practiced it, pared it down, punched it up. And now I finally have it down to fighting weight. Half a page of bullet points, with exhibits to match. When I arrive at the courthouse on the morning of closing arguments, the hallway is jammed to overflowing. There are members of the press and media—this case is front-page news—as well as my client's family members, corporate executives from the defendant companies, and scores of random spectators.

The pressure is on. This is a big one, and I need to hit a home run.

I head into the courtroom, dragging my usual boxes of trial materials, and sit down with my trial tech. I need to give him the outline of my closing argument so that he can display the exhibits in the correct order. When I go to grab my half page of bullet points, it's gone! I can't find it anywhere. Crap! I must have left it in my car. It'll take me fifteen minutes to get to my car and come back, and I can't afford to waste that much time.

I need those notes, though. I worked really hard on them. They're essential.

So I hurry back to my car. But the notes aren't there.

I'm on the verge of panic, working my way back through the crowd of news reporters, but I can't spend any more time on this. My only option is to rewrite my outline on the spot. My trial tech is anxiously awaiting my instructions as the audience fills the seats of the gallery and the jury is seated in the box. I barely have time to hand my tech a scrap of paper when the bailiff announces, "All rise!"

Judge Javitz enters the room and wastes no time turning the floor over to me. "All right, Ms. Barta, you may commence your closing argument."

I freeze for a moment, terrified that my hastily scribbled notes are going to fail me. And then I say to the jury, "Well, it seems like it's been about five years since the start of this trial."

The judge, for some reason, takes this as an accusation. "It has hardly been five years, Ms. Barta."

"Well, it may not feel like that from up there, Your Honor, but from down here it sure does."

This draws a laugh from the jurors, and I feel warmth emanating from them in a wave. That's all the boost I need to give me confidence. Before I know it, I'm off and running, and I don't even look at my scribbled notes . . .

33

Four hours later, Kurt Williams and I are sitting across from each other in the narrow hallway. I'm reading *Bon Appétit*—I'm a foodie, what can I say—and he's reading *Yachting World*. We're trying to avoid eye contact. Members of the media are milling about, talking and joking with one another, making phone calls.

There's a sudden hush as the court clerk steps out of the courtroom and hurries down the hall toward us. "The jury has reached a verdict," he says.

Stampede.

The jury has been asked two sets of questions in this case and will be polled in two phases. For phase one, the jury has been instructed to answer the following:

Did the defendant terminate the plaintiff?

If so, did the defendant act wrongfully?

Did the plaintiff suffer damages?

If so, what is the amount of those damages?

After everyone has filed into the courtroom, the judge thanks the jury for their service, confirms that true verdicts have been reached, and gives out some basic instructions as to who can leave the courtroom, when, and how, once the verdict has been read.

Then he announces, "This is a civil case, and, therefore, nine out of twelve jurors are required in order to reach agreement and answer each question. Will the jury foreman please stand?" The foreman stands. "As I read the verdicts," says Javitz, "along with the polling numbers of the jurors, will you please confirm the results?"

"Yes, Your Honor," says the foreman.

"As to question number one, 'Did the defendant terminate the plaintiff's employment?' the jury found yes, by unanimous count."

"That is correct, Your Honor."

"As to question number two, 'Did the defendant act wrongfully in terminating the plaintiff?' the jury found yes, by a count of ten out of twelve."

"That is correct, Your Honor."

"Question number three, 'Did the plaintiff suffer damages as a result of this termination?' the jury found yes, by a count of nine out of twelve."

"Correct, Your Honor."

"And finally, question number four, 'What is the amount of these damages?' the jury decided, for economic damages, on a figure of $125,000, by a count of eleven out of twelve."

"Yes, that's correct, Your Honor."

Steve sighs. He is clearly disappointed in the figure. "Wait," I whisper to him.

Judge Javitz continues. "The jury also decided that there were noneconomic damages based on emotional distress and damage to the plaintiff's reputation, did it not?"

"Yes, Your Honor," replies the foreman.

"And the amount of those noneconomic damages was set by the jury as . . . ?"

The micropause before he announces the dollar figure seems to stretch on to infinity.

"$1.5 million, is that correct?"

"It is, Your Honor," states the foreman, flashing just a hint of a smile at Steve and me.

Steve clutches my hand in disbelief. It's not good form to react too strongly to a verdict in civil court, but I can feel a flood of emotion being unleashed in that simple touch.

"Now we come to the second phase of the verdict," says the judge. "The punitive aspect. Here, the burden of proof is higher than simple 'preponderance of evidence.' In order to find a defendant liable for punitive damages, there must be 'clear and convincing proof.'"

The jury has been asked to answer three questions for phase two:

Did the defendant act with malice?

Did the defendant act with oppression?

Did the defendant act with fraud?

"In order for the court to levy punitive damages," Javitz explains, "the jury must find a yes answer to at least one of these questions, by a count of nine out of twelve." It's hard to guess how the jury will have voted here, especially since they weren't unanimous about the wrongdoing, the damages, or the amount of the damages.

That's why the answers to the phase two questions are doubly surprising.

Javitz announces, "As to question number one, 'Did the defendant act with malice?' the jury found yes, by unanimous count."

"That is correct, Your Honor."

"As to question number two, 'Did the defendant act with oppression?' the jury found yes, by unanimous count."

"That is correct, Your Honor."

"As to question number three, 'Did the defendant act with fraud?' the jury found yes, by unanimous count."

"That is correct, Your Honor."

34

I can't believe my ears. Even though the jurors were far from unanimous on the questions of wrongdoing and damages, they somehow came to unanimous agreement on the issues relating to punitive damages. Odd. But wonderful.

This means that punitive damages *will* be awarded.

The judge now explains that the jury is to go home and return in two days for the hearing on damages. He explains that when they reconvene, they will be shown evidence of the defendant's net worth, and the plaintiff's and defendant's attorneys will argue as to what the amount of punitive damages should be. And then the jury will decide.

One of the main reasons the court schedules the punitive damages hearing on a separate day is to give the parties an opportunity to settle. And this is what, in fact, happens almost every time. Defense attorneys and their clients, as a rule, do not want the jury to award punitive damages, especially when jurors have reached unanimous findings of malice, oppression, *and* fraud. They know that when a jury awards punitive damages, the figure can be ten or twenty (or even more) times higher than the actual damages.

And so, as I'm leaving the courtroom, I am not surprised when Kurt Williams catches my eye and says, "Can we talk?"

We schedule a settlement meeting for the following morning. When we get together, the defense makes its "first offer," a low-seven-figure amount that I know they're expecting me to counter. But Steve surprises me by urging me to accept the offer. In fact, he tells me, he's not comfortable accepting more than the offered amount. He reminds me of what I knew all along: this really wasn't about the money for him. This was about Steve's right to practice medicine as his conscience and professional standards dictated, without being unfairly punished for it. He feels vindicated now. His reputation will be restored, and he will have plenty of money to enjoy a comfortable retirement in a few years' time. He wasn't out for vengeance, only justice.

So the case result is a win/win/win. Steve gets what he wanted and is compensated fairly for his termination. I get a happy client and a court victory. And even the defendant is happy. They know we could have demanded a lot more money, and they must be feeling tremendous relief at our first-offer acceptance.

But still, this trial has cost them, publicly and privately. Maybe next time they won't be so quick to fire a good doctor and play dice with the lives of innocent patients.

PART IV

A Dermatologist's Tale

Doctor and Patient

35

Rose looked around at the waiting room crowd. Standing room only. At ten in the morning. *How are the doctors going to see all these people?* she wondered idly. She'd been told by the medical group to arrive half an hour early to fill out "new patient paperwork." She had finished filling out the forms, and now she was staring at some canned show called "AccentHealth" on the waiting room TV. But she wasn't really seeing a damned thing. All of her thoughts were on the moles on her neck.

She had several of them, mostly small. But two of them were *not* small, not anymore; they were getting bigger. They were also changing color, darkening. Her dad had received a cancer diagnosis some years earlier, and she herself had had a precancerous mole removed not too long ago. So she was concerned. She knew that time could be a critical factor when it came to treating skin cancer.

Therein lay her main concern. Today's appointment was not even with a dermatologist. She had wanted to see a skin specialist directly, but her insurance company told her she needed to see a "family doctor" first. Not even *her* family doctor—he wasn't in her provider network anymore—but just a doctor who practiced "family medicine" within the medical group she was assigned to.

Now it was up to *this* doctor to decide if she should see a dermatologist. And if so, that would mean another wait for another appointment. More time wasted.

And what if I don't have time to spare?

A young man dressed in nurse's blues popped his head out of the treatment area and called out, "Rose Stevens."

This young man, who looked like he was about twelve, took Rose's vital signs and weighed her while asking her questions about seemingly unrelated health issues and typing her answers into a tablet computer. He finally asked Rose why she was here today—almost as an after-thought—and she explained, "I'm concerned about a couple of moles on my neck; they're getting bigger and darker and I have a family history of skin cancer."

The young man hurriedly typed the information into his device without looking at her. Everyone who worked here seemed to be in such a rush.

When a woman with a stethoscope around her neck came into the room to see her next, Rose thought she was the doctor, but she turned out to be a medical assistant. She fired off almost the exact same questions the "boy in blue" had, quickly typing the answers into a laptop, presumably recording them in Rose's electronic medical record (her EMR). This woman also asked Rose why she was here today. Again Rose explained about the changing look of the moles on her neck. Again the staffer typed.

A little aside here from the author. If you've ever wondered why so many people ask you so many questions in doctors' offices nowadays, a lot of it comes down to something called hierarchical condition category (HCC) coding. It's all about billing. If a patient shows up for an acute issue, such as flu symptoms, and also turns out to have a chronic condition, such as high blood pressure or high cholesterol, the health plan or insurance company may pay extra. Why? Because the case is considered more complex. That's why they always ask about any other conditions you might have, and why they document it so carefully. It's more about coding and reimbursement than your health care. Sorry.

When the doctor finally came in, he said, "I'm Dr. Dowd," and hurried over to the wheeling stand where the laptop rested, barely looking at Rose. He immediately began scanning the screen, asking some of the same questions the previous two staffers had asked. He, too, seemed hurried and distracted. At last he strode across the room and took a brisk look at her moles.

"Moles are common, and almost everyone has them," he said. "Some people just have more than others. There's really nothing to worry about, but if they change shape or color, or grow larger, come back and see me."

Rose wanted to explain that that was exactly why she was there—because the moles *had* grown and they *were* getting darker—but she had already told that to the two staffers, and both had typed that information into the computer. So she assumed the doctor already knew those facts, and she didn't want to appear to be questioning his judgment. Some doctors were testy that way, she knew.

As Rose headed out of the lobby toward her car, her gut was telling her that she hadn't really been heard in there. She was afraid that if the right diagnosis wasn't made, she might be setting her treatment back by weeks. And she might be missing the ideal window for optimal treatment results.

A doctor did examine you, she reminded herself. *He'd have noticed if there was anything to worry about. Right?*

36

Dr. Ira Dowd was not a careless doctor. In fact, he thought of himself as a very conscientious one. This hurried, impersonal style of seeing patients was not how he had been trained in medical school, and it certainly was not how he had practiced when he started his medical career twenty-two years ago. He often longed for the old days again—the days when his patients were scheduled twenty or thirty minutes apart. Nowadays, when he opened his schedule screen each morning, he saw three names next to each fifteen-minute slot. Triple booking, they called it.

Why so many patients, all day long, from 8:00 a.m. to 5:30 p.m.?

The term the management team tossed around was "through-put," or TP. It referred to the total elapsed time between a patient's signing in and exiting the door. The bosses were forever stressing the importance of faster and faster TP. They made it sound very patient friendly: "The way to provide greater patient access is to make a lot of appointments available. The faster the TP, the more patients we can see."

But Ira Dowd wasn't stupid. He knew that faster TP meant more billings for the medical group. And to keep up with the demand, he was constantly rushed, constantly falling behind.

The ones who suffered the most were the patients. It just wasn't possible to give them the time they deserved with a triple-booked schedule. If you have three patients to see every fifteen minutes, and you're supposed to give each of them ten minutes, well, that's just not possible without rewriting the laws of physics. But of course you weren't supposed to bring that up with the bosses. The unspoken message was that any doctor who couldn't keep up with the workload could be easily replaced.

He hated the relentless pace, but he needed the job. He had three kids—one already in college and twins who would start next year—plus a mortgage, car payments, and an endless stream of bills to pay each month. He knew that doctors could no longer survive financially by working for themselves, so he needed to work for a large group. And all of the large medical groups were becoming increasingly similar in terms of their demands.

Ira Dowd still loved practicing medicine—meeting with patients, figuring out the best treatment options, and helping them heal. But he wished he could practice the way he had been trained.

When he walked into Exam Room F, the woman—he glanced at her name on the chart but quickly forgot it—seemed nice enough. But he didn't have time for chitchat this morning. Only two hours into his day, he'd already seen fourteen patients and was four behind.

The woman was talking, but Ira was focused on the computer screen. He knew he could gather information more efficiently there. He was trying to figure out why she was here and what information he would need to input in the system.

He hated the new EMR system. It required him to enter so much data that he had to repeatedly scroll through various screens, which kept him glued to the computer instead of focused on the patient. How was he supposed to "observe" his patients—observation being the cornerstone of diagnosis—when he only had a few rushed minutes with each of them, and spent most of that time interfacing with a machine?

The woman was presenting with concerns about "moles." She really should be seeing a dermatologist, *Ira thought.* But he knew that that would only happen if he referred her to one. Patients had to see their PCP first and then get a referral to see a specialist. And the company frowned on referrals. Why? Because they meant more money spent on more doctors. Even though Ira Dowd was not specifically trained in the diagnosis of skin cancer, he was the only doctor this woman would *see—unless he was willing to stick his neck out and refer her to a dermatologist.*

When it came to referrals, he had to pick his battles. He recalled the PowerPoint presentation at the physicians' meeting last month. "Leakage" was what the administration called it when the company spent money on outside referrals. Leakage was considered bad. The company kept track of how many outside referrals each doctor made, and doctors were "encouraged" to keep their numbers down. The bottom line: Dr. Dowd had to save his referrals for the truly challenging and life-threatening cases.

He decided this woman's moles did not cross the threshold for a referral. So he rattled off his general spiel about moles, encouraging her to "come back and see me" if they changed or grew bigger.

He left the room without making eye contact with the woman. He wasn't being rude; the truth was that he felt a ping of shame at the way he'd had to treat her. But this was how he had to practice medicine today.

37

Dr. Dowd's diagnosis—or lack thereof—didn't sit well with Rose. Something told her the moles just "didn't look right"—they were too dark and too weird in shape. Her previous research, as well as her experience with her dad, told her that these were not good signs.

On the other hand, she didn't want to be one of *those* patients who worry so much about "symptoms" that they literally *create* the very diagnoses they fear.

Maybe things had changed in skin cancer treatment over the last few years. She decided to research the topic afresh. What she discovered on the medical websites was the opposite of reassuring. Holy cow, the moles on her neck fit *all*—not just one or two—of the criteria for cancerous moles.

"I'm really worried," she told her husband, Dan, after an evening of Web surfing. "Scared, actually. Every Web article about cancerous moles describes mine to a T."

"You've got to see a specialist, sweetie. Someone trained in diagnosing and treating skin cancer."

"I don't know if we're covered under our plan. I think the PCP has to make a referral for something like that."

"You need to go see a specialist, covered or not," said Dan.

"We can't afford it. Not on top of what we already pay for the freaking premiums every month. Also, if I don't go through the proper channels for the initial visit, they might deny all my follow-up treatment."

The next day, Rose tried to figure out what was and wasn't covered under her health insurance plan. She ended up more confused than ever. The brochure said she needed a referral to see a specialist; the website said she *didn't* need a referral to see any doctor who was listed in the provider network directory.

She'd found a dermatologist, Dr. Mangini, who specialized in skin cancer and was in the provider network. So did she need a referral or not? Every time she called the insurance company to find out, she was put on hold for the length of a minor ice age and then had to wend her way through a maze of digital menus, none of which offered the option she was looking for. After a "please press three," a "please press six," and a "please press one," she inevitably ended up at the recording that said, "Please consult your policy for any questions you have about coverage."

She was utterly confused about how her new "EPO" coverage worked.

But one thing she wasn't confused about was her moles. They were getting darker and larger, she was sure of it. She kept trying to convince herself that she was just being an alarmist because of her father's diagnosis. But every night, she awoke in a panic in the predawn hours. Her panic did not dissipate by daylight. Whenever she looked at her neck in the mirror, she was convinced she had reason for worry.

Enough was enough. She called the dermatology practice where Dr. Mangini worked and made an appointment.

38

Dr. Tina Mangini was young, but Rose liked and trusted her immediately. Her manner was attentive, caring. In many ways, she was more "old school" than some of the older doctors Rose had seen. What Rose liked about her the most was that she did a biopsy on her mole right then and there.

She'd had a mole removed three years earlier by a different doctor, but that time she'd had to schedule a second appointment to have the biopsy performed. It wasn't so much the inconvenience of missing work a second time that had irked her; it was the two-week wait for the procedure and the worry that came along with it. That time, she'd been lucky; the mole cells had been precancerous, and the doctor had been able to remove them before any trouble could start. This time, who knew? She was glad she wouldn't have to wait too long to find out.

Dr. Mangini promised Rose she would personally call her as soon as she had the biopsy results. And the office staff assured her that her visit was indeed covered under her EPO plan. She left Dr. Mangini's office feeling apprehensive but confident in her new doctor and team.

The news was not good.

Dr. Mangini did indeed call Rose herself, rather than having a nurse or staff person deliver the news. It was after hours, so Rose knew she was missing out on her own family time to make the call.

"I'm afraid the biopsy came up positive," she explained in her gentle manner. "We detected a carcinoma there."

Rose shrieked and burst into tears, but Dr. Mangini hung in there with her.

"The good news—and it's *very* good news—is that we caught it early," she said. "That leaves us some excellent treatment options with some very high success rates."

Rose asked what treatment she was referring to, and she explained, "I'd like to perform a procedure known as Mohs surgery—not 'moles' but Mohs, M-o-h-s."

"What's that?" asked Rose, through her tears.

"It's less invasive than the typical 'cut and dig' procedure, but equally effective. *More* effective, in fact, statistically speaking. We remove the tissue in very thin layers, taking only the minimum amount necessary to purge the cancerous cells. That way, we preserve the greatest possible amount of healthy tissue. The side benefit is that, cosmetically speaking, we end up with a much nicer result as well. Odds are, if we do this procedure, you're going to be just fine, Rose."

Rose immediately agreed to the procedure, and Dr. Mangini gave her the earliest possible appointment, which was just a few days away.

Rose was delighted with the outcome, not only because the cancer was gone but also because she barely had a scar. The moles had been on the front and side of her neck. She was happy she would not be the recipient of awkward stares for the rest of her life.

About six weeks after the surgery, when she had put the whole experience behind her and moved on with her life, a letter arrived. It was from her insurance company—we'll call it Omega Health—and it read, "We have denied payment on this claim because a medical director and/or physician has determined that the services you received were not medically necessary."

Rose stared at the paper in stunned disbelief. *What? Not medically necessary? How can this be? Dr. Mangini said the moles were cancerous and that the surgery was needed to remove them.*

39

Dr. Tina Mangini received her notice from Omega around the same time Rose did. The insurer's thumbs-down was galling to her, though far from surprising. Even though Mohs surgery had become the gold standard for treating several forms of skin cancer, and even though the insurance companies had approved most of the Mohs surgeries Tina had performed in her first couple of years of practice, Omega was now rejecting more and more of them. Why? It was the same medical procedure, with the same medical need. And the statistics for its success rates had actually improved over the last couple of years. Tina was getting angrier about these rejections by the day.

Tina loved practicing medicine. Her father and uncle had both been doctors, and Tina had wanted to be one as far back as she could remember. Her interest eventually gravitated toward dermatology, medical dermatology in particular—the treatment of skin disorders and diseases. Tina was drawn to the life-enhancing aspects of this practice. Whereas many medical issues are internal to the body, skin disorders are visible to the world and often lead to emotional distress and an erosion of self-esteem.

And so she was excited to be practicing this specialty. Her expertise was in laser treatment of rosacea and in Mohs surgery for skin cancer. Both of these procedures not only treated the disease but also improved aesthetic appearance for patients.

Dr. M always did what she felt was best for her patients. She enjoyed meeting new patients and taking time with her old ones to talk about their lives and families. She had been warned in medical school that "medicine was changing"—that it was becoming more about the numbers than about personal relationships with patients.

But Tina Mangini didn't practice that way. She spent time with each of her patients and took their feelings into account. For example, if she found a mole concerning, she biopsied it immediately. And when the pathology results came in, she personally called the patient if the news was not good. She routinely spent her lunch hour, evenings, and Saturdays talking to her patients, consoling them, and discussing treatment options.

Needless to say, she found this growing trend of insurers denying payments highly disconcerting. She believed the insurer was impairing her ability to provide good health care for her patients. And so she fought back. She appealed and disputed the insurer's decisions. She wrote letters. She called and argued with the insurer. She even attended in-person meetings with the company's medical directors, which meant taking time away from her practice to drive—in Los Angeles traffic—to the insurer's corporate offices.

Tina read Rose's denial notice again, sat down at her computer, loaded up the "appeal" form template, and started typing furiously.

40

Rose began to wonder, *Had Dr. Mangini really performed a surgery that wasn't necessary?* Here was another doctor saying so, in black and white, right on her denial notice. Maybe she should have sought a second opinion before undergoing the procedure. But she had trusted Dr. M. She had seemed so capable and knowledgeable. But then again, wasn't that always the way a con man *seemed*?

According to the Web research she'd done, Dr. M was well qualified and had all the proper certifications. And the surgery had gone well, as far as she knew. The cancer was gone, and her neck showed almost no evidence that it had ever existed. Still . . . she felt duped, used. If Dr. M had really performed a surgery that was "not medically necessary," then she must be either a bad doctor or a sleazy one who liked to bill insurance companies fraudulently.

The only silver lining was that the notice from Omega said she was not responsible for paying the bill, since her doctor had told her the procedure was necessary. Still, she didn't like the idea of playing lab rat to an overzealous practitioner. Rose called Dr. Mangini's office immediately and asked to speak with her about the issue. She was directed to someone in the billing office.

"We're aware of the situation, Mrs. Stevens, and we've already sent an appeal of your denial to the insurance company. I can tell you personally that Dr. Mangini was very upset about this. She is confident the decision will be reversed on appeal, but it might take several months. In the meantime, try not to worry about it. You were in good hands with Dr. M, and you still are."

This reassured Rose slightly, but when she hung up, there was still doubt in her mind. *If the procedure had been medically necessary, the insurance company would surely have paid for it.*

In just one month's time, Dr. Mangini wrote appeal letters for twenty different rosacea and Mohs surgery patients whose claims had been rejected by Omega. It was time-consuming work that ate up her weekend and evening hours. In each appeal letter, she painstakingly detailed the patient's medical history, diagnosis, and individual need for the treatment. She then summarized each procedure and explained the positive results for each patient, even making the effort to include photos.

When Tina received twenty identical form letters from Omega rejecting each of her carefully crafted appeals, she was furious. She called and demanded to speak with the head medical director. "Someone will call you back," she was told.

They didn't.

She called Omega again and was told again that someone would call her. This time she said, "I'll hold. Please put someone on the phone now.*" She was on hold for over thirty minutes, and then the phone disconnected. She called right back, but she was, of course, connected to a different person, and she had to start the cycle all over. Again she was placed on hold. And again, after more than thirty minutes of hold time, the phone disconnected.*

Furious, Tina called a lawyer her medical group used for reviewing insurance company contracts and asked for help. The lawyer wrote to Omega stating that Dr. Mangini was demanding the company conduct a so-called "meet-and-confer"—an in-person review—on all twenty of these denied claims.

It took almost two months of back-and-forth letters for the meet-and-confer to be set up. Tina had to take the afternoon off from her practice and drive for over an hour to Omega's corporate offices. She arrived armed with case files. Her lawyer met her in the parking lot, and together they walked into the towering eighteen-story building (built on the profits of unpaid medical claims, reflected Tina).

After passing through a security system that rivaled LAX's, Dr. M and her attorney were escorted to a large conference room. Seated at a massive table, one that probably cost two months of Tina's income, were three men and one woman, all in suits. Two were attorneys, and two were medical directors employed by Omega.

The meeting lasted less than forty-five minutes. During the first fifteen of those, Stephanie Atwood, one of Omega's lawyers, explained the "rules" of the meet-and-confer in depth. When she saw the digital recorder Tina's lawyer had brought along, she said, "Oh, and another rule, no recording."

At last she announced, "Let's begin. You have fifteen minutes total to make your case. And you will be timed."

"Fifteen minutes? For all twenty cases?" stammered Tina in disbelief. "That's forty-five seconds per patient. You're joking, right?"

41

Evidently, Atwood wasn't joking. Tina was about to protest the absurdity of the situation, but then realized she would only be wasting valuable time.

Because she had already explained her reasoning for the medical procedures in great detail in the twenty individual letters she had submitted, she decided not to retread old turf here. Instead, she looked at the two medical directors and asked them point blank, "Is this about money? Is that the real reason these treatments are being denied?"

The medical directors did not reply, just glared at her icily.

OK, *Tina thought.* Time for a different tack. *Tina held up before-and-after photos of some of her patients and tried to explain the psychological effects of having a disfiguring skin condition such as rosacea or surgical scars. She emphasized how depression, suicidal thinking, social withdrawal, anger, and low self-esteem were higher among skin-disorder sufferers than among the general population. She talked about how patients with visible skin conditions face higher rates of unemployment and are often forced to dress differently and change their lifestyle habits.*

Attorney Atwood cut her off mid-sentence. "Your fifteen minutes is up. Now it's time for the medical directors to respond."

Only one of the men spoke, a Dr. Baldwin. He looked to be about eighty years old. "I reviewed your letters and the medical records," he said with a note of irritation in his voice, "and the treatments simply were not medically necessary—they were for cosmetic purposes."

"What is your expertise and medical background?" Dr. M challenged him. "Are you a dermatologist? Have you ever treated a patient with rosacea?"

"*Irrelevant,*" *chimed in one of the attorneys.* "*You don't need to respond.*"

But the medical director chose to answer anyway. With pride, he declared, "*I practiced medicine for over thirty years.*"

"*In what field?*" *Dr. Mangini asked.*

"*I was a physiatrist,*" *replied Baldwin.*

Unbelievable, *thought Dr. M.* A physiatrist is a "rehabilitation and pain management" physician. Nothing to do with skin pathologies.

"*Was?*" *replied Dr. M.* "*When was the last time you actually treated a patient?*"

Again, Dr. Baldwin answered with seemingly clueless pride. "*I retired from seeing patients twenty-two years ago.*"

So my medical treatments are being denied by a doctor who hasn't seen a patient in over twenty years and has no expertise in dermatology, skin disorders, or the latest forms of treatment, *Tina realized.*

Tina challenged the second medical director, a man named Dr. Valcourt, as she had the first one. "*What about you? Have you ever treated a patient with rosacea or skin cancer? What's your medical specialty? When's the last time you treated a patient?*"

Valcourt, also an elderly man, stood up and said, "*That's none of your business, frankly. I've reviewed the appeals you submitted, and the treatment you provided was not medically necessary, period.*"

Just as Valcourt was about to storm out of the room, Dr. M looked him in the eye and said, "*You're no doctor. You're just a figurehead. Your only job is to save Omega money.*"

42

It took only a week for Omega to strike back. Dr. M was notified that she had been placed on "prepayment review," or PPR, which meant that before Omega would process any claim from her, she now had to send in medical records supporting the services she had provided. This process required reams of extra paperwork for Tina.

Omega also sent automatically generated letters to each of her patients who had claims pending, stating, "The services you received from Dr. Mangini are being reviewed to determine whether they were medically necessary." This blanket warning caused Dr. M's patients to doubt her medical ability and her billing practices.

Omega did not give Dr. M a reason for placing her on PPR—although it wasn't hard to figure it out, given the timing—but Tina wanted it in writing. After she'd demanded a written justification several times, Omega finally sent her a letter stating that the company had discovered an investigation of Mangini by the California Department of Insurance. This was news to Tina.

While on PPR, Dr. M continued to treat her patients and to bill Omega. Every single claim was dutifully "reviewed" by the insurer. Some claims were actually paid, but those payments took months.

The majority of the claims, however, were denied. More letters were sent to Dr. M's patients, stating, "The services Dr. Mangini provided were not medically necessary." This meant Omega was not paying for services. But Omega took things a step further. Each rejection letter to patients also stated, "Because the services were not medically necessary, you are not responsible for paying for the services."

The problem with that statement—besides the fact that it crippled Tina's ability to collect any payment for her services—was that it was blatantly false. While Omega may have been legally entitled to refuse paying benefits for any services it deemed "not medically necessary," nowhere in the policies—or the law—was there language stating that the patient, therefore, had no responsibility to pay. As a result of what Omega was telling patients, however, Dr. M was unable to get paid at all for the services that Omega refused to cover. Tina felt certain this was a retaliatory attempt by Omega to cause her financial harm.

But she soldiered on, continuing to appeal each and every denied claim. This was starting to cost her a fortune. Not only was she providing services she wasn't getting paid for, but she also had to hire more staff to handle all the paperwork. She could barely keep up. But she forced herself to do so. She knew Omega was trying to bully her into stopping her treatments altogether, and she refused to be cowed into submission.

This went on for many months, and then Omega upped the stakes again. One day, all of the doctors in Dr. M's medical group received letters stating they were being placed on "prepayment review." Again, no justification or reason was given.

Dr. M had had enough. She wrote a letter to Omega accusing the insurance company of retaliating against her and interfering with her practice of medicine. She stated that, in her opinion, Omega's motivation stemmed from "a desire to reduce claims payments and not from a genuine question over the medical necessity of the treatment or concern for patient welfare." She ended the letter with, "I refuse to compromise the standard of care required by my patients simply because you, Omega Health, refuse to reimburse for those services. If you do not cease and desist with your retaliatory conduct, I will sue."

Omega did not respond to Dr. M's letter. But one month later, the company terminated Dr. M from its provider network. Again, no reason was offered. Although Tina wasn't exactly shocked, she was devastated. Over half of her patients were insured with Omega. This meant that she would lose all of those patients, as well as any future patients who had Omega as their insurer. That would be a huge blow to her practice.

Little did Tina know, her troubles were only going to snowball from there.

Tina was contracted with several other major insurers in addition to Omega, and was part of their provider networks too. To remain in good standing with these insurers, she had to "recredential" with each of them every year or two. That meant she had to complete a questionnaire that asked, among other things, whether she had ever been terminated by any other health plan. She was now required to answer yes to this question—which in turn became a reason for each of the other insurers to drop her. One by one, each insurer notified her that her participation in their provider network was not being renewed. No reason was ever given, but since she had no other black marks against her, the reason was obvious.

She had been blackballed. Since she was a young physician, this could be career ending.

43

The appeal of Rose's case was finally resolved. It had taken months, but in the end, the insurance company did pay for the procedure. Obviously, Dr. Mangini had not performed any "unnecessary" services. Rose was happy about this, because in her heart she had believed that Dr. M was a good doctor and a good person.

So a year later, when she saw a strange spot on her chest growing larger and darker just as the two moles on her neck had done, she called Dr. Mangini's office to make an appointment. To her dismay, she was told that Dr. M was no longer taking insurance—not just her insurance, *any* insurance. She didn't blame Dr. Mangini for getting out of the insurance game, given how Omega had treated her. But now what was she going to do?

Her only option was to go back to square one. She had to call for an appointment with a family doctor at the big group practice. Not a skin cancer specialist. Not even a dermatologist. Not a doctor who knew her or cared about her. And to top it off, the scheduling person on the phone said, "The next available appointment is in two months." Rose knew that, when it came to skin cancer, two months could be an eternity. Literally.

By the time her appointment rolled around, she wasn't even focused on the moles. She had a nasty cold that had settled in her chest, and she wasn't feeling up to going to the doctor at all. She'd been coughing for weeks now; she felt tired and run down; all she wanted to do was stay in bed. She'd had chest colds before, and she knew they sometimes lingered. But not like this. Not for this long. This had been going on for weeks.

She hated coming to this medical practice; it was not a warm, caring place like Dr. M's office. It was a mill. The driving principle seemed to be, *How many patients can we cram in, and how quickly can we shuffle them in and out the door?* She felt more like a number than a human being here—a medical ID number, to be exact. The ID number was printed on everything at this clinic. When she checked in and wrote her name on the sign-in sheet, the receptionist put a bright sticker with her ID number on it right beside it. When the nursing staff brought out her patient's file, the ID number was displayed in big, bright colors on the folder, her name in small print.

After waiting for thirty minutes, Rose was led to a room by a man who didn't even look up from the paperwork he was carrying. He simply came out to the waiting room, called three names, and then led all three patients down a hallway, pointing each to a room to sit in. She went into her assigned room and closed the door herself.

After about five minutes, the door opened, and a woman strode in. She said hello and went straight to the computer. As with Rose's previous visit, the woman asked a bunch of questions, typing as she went, never looking at Rose. Then, as suddenly as she had come in, the woman departed, saying, "The doctor will be in shortly."

After another ten minutes, the doctor finally came in. He also made a beeline for the computer and started typing.

"I'm Dr. Mukherjee," he said eventually. "So what brings you in today?"

"Well, I originally scheduled the appointment because I was concerned about a spot on my chest, but now I have this terrible cough that won't go away."

"I can only address one of your concerns today."

"What?" said Rose. She thought she'd heard him incorrectly.

"Our billing policy permits us to look at only one 'med problem' per visit. You'll have to make a separate appointment for the second complaint."

Rose was so sure he was joking, she laughed aloud.

The doctor did not share her sense of humor. He simply stared at her and said, "Which of your concerns would you like me to check on today?"

My God, he's serious, she thought. *What has the practice of medicine come to? And why is he asking* me *this question? He's the doctor. Shouldn't he know which symptom is the more urgent one? And what if, heaven forbid, the two symptoms are related? What do we do then?*

"I guess I'm more concerned about the spot on my chest," said Rose.

"And why is that?"

"Because I was treated for melanoma about a year ago."

The doctor frowned at this, showing his first real sign of life and interest. He examined the spot on her chest and seemed to become concerned himself.

Like Dr. Dowd—the first "family" doctor Rose had seen—Dr. Mukherjee wanted to order some immediate tests for Rose, but he knew that tests were discouraged by his bosses. Mukherjee had received a "profile" from an insurer and had been threatened with being placed on prepayment review (PPR). A couple of his friends and colleagues had been placed on PPR, and he'd seen what had happened to their practices. Their claims began to be denied, and their patients were told that their treatment was "not medically necessary." Those doctors eventually couldn't even pay their overhead.

Mukherjee couldn't afford to have that happen to him. Still, he felt a surge of anger about the situation he was in. He shouldn't be seeing dermatology patients to begin with—and if he was required to do so, he ought to be free to order whatever tests he saw fit.

He decided not to order tests, but he knew he needed to do something for this patient.

"I want you to be seen by a specialist," Dr. Mukherjee said to Rose, and he made a referral to one of the dermatologists within the group.

When Rose went to make the appointment, of course, it was scheduled another month away.

44

Rose didn't last a week. A few days after her visit with Dr. Mukherjee, she awoke feeling as if she'd been run over by a train. Her chest hurt—even when she wasn't coughing—she felt weak, and there were large, painful lumps in her neck and under her arms. She knew she couldn't wait for an appointment at the regular clinic, so she drove to the urgent care facility a few miles from her house.

The doctor at the urgent care center was a tall, personable man with kind eyes. He sat down across from her and actually looked into her eyes as she described her symptoms. He never looked at a computer. He asked if she had been sick in the past or had any other medical concerns. She gave him her history and showed him the spot on her chest. He ordered a chest X-ray to be done right there on the spot.

Within an hour of her arrival, the urgent care physician sat down with Rose again.

"I'm afraid I have some troubling news, Rose. I reviewed your X-ray. I was concerned about what I saw, so I e-mailed your pictures to an oncologist I know and asked her to take a look."

"And . . . ?"

"I just got off the phone with her. She confirmed what I thought I was seeing. The spot on your chest is a melanoma, and it has metastasized to your lungs. That's why you've been coughing the way you have."

Rose was in shock. She thought back to her appointment with Dr. Mukherjee and how he had ignored her cough because it was considered a "second" medical issue. She wondered if the metastasis could have been averted had she not been made to wait two months before seeing Dr. Mukherjee. She remembered Dr. Mangini explaining how the successful treatment of melanoma depended on how quickly it was discovered.

Dr. Tina Mangini came into her office on Tuesday morning to find a note from her assistant. One of her prior patients, Rose Stevens, had been diagnosed with metastatic lung cancer, and her oncologist had called asking for copies of Dr. M's medical records.

Tina remembered Rose and how she'd had a family history of skin cancer. When she had come to see Tina, it was because a "family doctor" at a large medical practice had failed to properly diagnose her moles. Fortunately for Rose, she had been alert enough to seek out a skin cancer specialist. And Dr. M had caught the problem in a timely way.

This time, however, it seemed Rose hadn't been so lucky. She had not made it in to see a dermatologist in time, and the melanoma had taken quickly to her lymph system and then gone straight for her lungs. Tina felt absolutely sick for her.

*What made her even sicker, though, was the fact that Rose could have come to her directly if she hadn't been blackballed by Omega. The insur-*ance company's retaliatory games might have cost this woman her life, *Tina realized. She wasn't going to stand for it any longer.*

PART V

A Dermatologist's Tale

The Lawsuit

45

Dr. Tina Mangini had already talked to three lawyers by the time she called me and asked to meet. She'd been told by these lawyers that she didn't have a case because her contract with Omega clearly stated that the contract could be severed with sixty days' notice and without cause. In other words, Omega didn't *have* to give a reason for terminating her. And Tina had agreed to that condition by signing the contract. Case closed.

Dr. M still felt strongly that she had been wronged, though, so she went to her medical group's business attorney, Mark Fowler—the same attorney who'd accompanied her to the meet-and-confer. Fowler believed Tina had a case. Fowler wasn't a litigator, though, so he did some research and found me.

I met with Tina and Mark at Fowler's office on a Saturday morning. Unlike many of the doctors who come to me, Tina didn't have to be talked into going after the insurer. She *wanted* to fight; she *wanted* to sue. She hoped I could help. As I always do, I asked Dr. M why *she* thought she had been terminated. (The termination letter gave no reason, but there is always a "reason.")

"Retaliation, pure and simple," said Dr. M. "After they denied payment to twenty plus of my most deserving patients and then denied my appeals, I asked Mark here to set up a meet-and-confer with them."

"At the meeting," added Attorney Fowler, "Tina called them out on their credentials and their judgment. They didn't like it, and they didn't like Tina."

"A week later, they put me on PPR, as punishment," said Dr. M, "and then they did the same to all of my colleagues. That's where I drew the line, and that's when I wrote this letter." She handed me the letter she had written, demanding that Omega take her off PPR and "cease and desist" its retaliatory actions.

"Three weeks later—surprise, surprise—I get a notice of termination."

The timing of Omega's actions strongly suggested to me that I was looking at a familiar pattern of retaliation by an insurance company. A few possible legal claims were starting to take shape in my mind— retaliation, wrongful termination, defamation. Why defamation? Well, those letters to patients stating that Dr. M had performed services "that were not medically necessary" were clearly harmful to Dr. M's reputation; they implied that she was either a bad doctor or was attempting to defraud an insurer by performing and billing for services that were not needed.

I also thought a strong argument could be made that Omega had interfered with Dr. M's ability to practice medicine. By terminating her contract, which led directly to the termination of her contracts with other insurers, Omega had made it extremely difficult for Dr. M to continue to practice as a physician.

Was I worried about the contract Tina had signed? Yes and no. You see, what many people—including some attorneys, who should know better—don't realize is that contracts are not all-powerful. Just because you sign a contract doesn't mean you have given up all of your rights. There are limits—serious limits—as to what rights you can "sign away" or can be *asked* to sign away in a contract. Not everything in a contract is necessarily binding.

I told Dr. M that I thought she had a case and that I was willing to take it on.

46

Two critical things occurred immediately after we filed the lawsuit. The first was that, along with the lawsuit, I served a set of interrogatories. These are questions your opponent is required to answer under oath and penalty of perjury. I asked Omega to state the reason it had terminated Dr. Mangini. Omega's response was, "The termination was *without cause.*"

OK, I thought. *Play that game if you want.* I suspected there *was* a reason: retaliation. And I would try to convince a jury of that. Regardless of what a contract or a termination letter may say, jurors are not stupid. They understand the simple truth: no company takes an action without cause. There is *always* a cause, a reason. And unless Omega could offer a reason for terminating Dr. M that was more compelling than the retaliation motive I planned to paint for the jury, I felt the jury would believe *us.*

But here's the interesting twist. Even if Omega eventually did come up with a credible and justifiable reason for canceling Tina's contract, they had already given a sworn statement that the termination had been *without* cause. So they were already in a bit of a bind, truth-wise. And I hoped I could get a jury to see that.

The second thing that happened was that Omega's lawyers filed paperwork asking the judge to order us to arbitration instead of a jury trial. This is known as a motion to compel arbitration. The justification for their motion flowed from another provision in Dr. M's contract, one that stipulated that disputes between Dr. M and Omega had to be arbitrated. This provision might give us trouble.

Insurers love arbitration. Me, I hate it, and I try to avoid it for several reasons. One, it strips away the doctor's right to be heard by a jury and instead hands the reins of the case over, in most instances, to a retired judge who works for the AAA (American Arbitration Association). And the results of AAA arbitrations typically favor big businesses, corporations, and insurance companies. Why? One simple reason: corporations give AAA repeat business, whereas a solo plaintiff typically doesn't. So there's a subtle, built-in conflict of interest, and the cards are stacked against a private individual.

When arbitration decisions *do* go in the individual's favor, they are not typically very large, and punitive damages are rarely awarded. (And it's the punitive damages that discourage insurance companies from engaging in bad behavior.)

Another problem with arbitration, from my point of view as a litigator, is that the proceedings are usually confidential. So when a doctor challenges a big insurance company, his or her professional peers never find out about it, even if the doctor scores a huge victory. This confidentiality plays in the insurers' favor. It perpetuates the myth that big insurers are all-powerful and can't be challenged. On the other hand, when doctors see one of their peers publicly "take down" an insurer, it emboldens them to attempt the same.

Finally, the amount of discovery that can be conducted in an arbitration case is limited and subject to dispute. So, it is very, very hard to get to the bottom of what really happened. In a jury trial, the rules of discovery are broader and stronger.

I filed an "opposition" to Omega's motion—a written argument explaining to the court why I thought the arbitration clause should not be invoked. I offered several reasons, but the crux of my argument came down to two things:

The first was that the paragraph containing the arbitration agreement was "buried" on page forty-six of a fifty-eight-page contract. This fifty-eight-page contract was given to doctors on a "take it or leave it" basis; it was essentially nonnegotiable. This is called a *contract of adhesion*—one party sets forth all of the provisions, and the other party has to sign it as is or walk away—and that's typically considered "unconscionable."

The second was that the contract also said that "no punitive damages or other remedy" were available to the doctor; the only available remedy was "monetary compensation" for his or her losses. I argued that this provision ran contrary to the law because it took away doctors' legal rights.

I wish I had one more solid blow I could land, but this would have to do.

Now it was up to a judge in court to decide whether my arguments held water or whether we would be forced to arbitrate. In my gut, I felt it could go either way.

47

The judge denied Omega's motion to compel arbitration. We had won the right to a jury trial! This was a major early victory. Now it was time to dig into discovery.

As I began to do some in-depth research into the case, three main areas of focus emerged as critical: 1) the process by which Omega made "medical necessity" decisions, 2) the way Omega handled appeals, and 3) the reasons for Dr. M's termination.

For the sake of clarity, let's look at these issues one at a time.

First, we'll consider the "medical necessity" front. From what Tina had told me, I suspected something was amiss in the way the insurer made determinations of "medical necessity" in her particular cases. So in my first deposition, I questioned an Omega employee who'd been assigned to answer my questions about this topic. I asked her to explain the claims review process.

"It starts with a review of each claim by one of our 'nurse reviewers,'" the woman told me. "They're contracted employees who work from home."

"So a doctor doesn't do these reviews?"

"Not initially. But if the nurse reviewer believes the services are not medically necessary, that claim is 'flagged' and sent on to one of our medical directors."

"I see. And these 'medical directors' are physicians, is that correct?"

"Yes."

"And how is it determined which medical director will review which claims?" I asked.

"I try to assign the claim to whichever director has the expertise or specialty best suited to the case."

"So if the medical service a doctor provided was for, say, broken bones, you would send the claim to an orthopedist?"

"Ideally, yes."

"And what if no medical director is available in the particular specialty required?"

"Then the claim is just randomly assigned to any medical director. I try to spread out the work evenly, so that one medical director is not overloaded. "

"I see. So if no appropriate specialist is available, the assignment of the case is made on the basis of chance and availability, mainly?"

"Yes, that's correct."

"How many medical directors did Omega have on staff during the year in which Dr. Mangini's claims were denied?"

"I would say around fifteen."

"So over the course of a year, if hundreds of Dr. Mangini's claims were reviewed by your medical directors, statistically all or most of your medical directors should have reviewed some of Dr. M's claims. Is that right?"

"Yes, I'd agree with that."

I was asking this question because I knew that only two medical directors had appeared at Dr. M's meet-and-confer. One of them, I'd learned, had reviewed *all* of Tina's cases for medical necessity; the other had reviewed *all* of her appeals when her original requests were denied. And neither of them specialized in skin treatments. What I was trying to establish by my questioning was that Dr. M had been prejudicially singled out within Omega and that her claims had not been assigned for review on the basis of expertise, randomness, or "first availability." Rather, Dr. M had been targeted internally.

After the deposition, I obtained documents from Omega—which they refused to furnish at first, so I had to seek a court order—that confirmed that, indeed, all of Dr. M's cases had been reviewed by these same two doctors.

Something besides random chance was at play here. Omega was up to something sketchy it didn't want to admit to.

48

Now it was time to depose the two medical directors. I purposely scheduled their depositions on the same day, back to back, so that they wouldn't be able to confer with one another and adjust their answers accordingly.

The first one, the director who had done the initial assessments of medical necessity, was named Baldwin. Through my initial questioning of him, I was able to learn that:

Though he tried to position himself as an objective, independent expert, he actually worked for only one employer: Omega Health.

He had not practiced medicine—i.e., treated actual patients—in many, many years.

When determining the medical necessity of procedures, he reviewed only medical records. He never saw or spoke to the patient, and he never spoke to the treating doctor. All of his decisions were based on paperwork only.

His medical specialty was unrelated to dermatology. He was a physiatrist. Therefore, when making determinations of "medical necessity" in Dr. M's cases, he was operating outside his area of expertise.

And yet, he was the only doctor who had reviewed all of Dr. M's cases. Hmm. What was going on here?

Throughout the deposition, Dr. Baldwin answered my questions very defensively.

"Can you explain," I asked Baldwin, "why, if you did not have a specialty in dermatology, you were the only medical director assigned to review every single one of Dr. Mangini's hundreds of claims?"

"I'm not in charge of how claims are assigned. I just do my job, which is to review the claims that come across my desk effectively and conscientiously."

"I see. And do you believe you have the expertise to 'effectively and conscientiously' determine the medical necessity of treatments for rosacea and skin cancer?"

"I do."

"Based on what?"

"Excuse me?"

"I mean what sort of training and experience do you have in medical dermatology?"

He muttered something defensive and then said, "During my residency, I did a six-week rotation through dermatology."

"And when did you do that residency, Dr. Baldwin?"

He thought for a moment and then defiantly spat out a range of years.

"That was about forty-seven years ago, isn't that right?"

"You seem to be the math expert; why don't you figure it out? "

"And during your brief exposure to dermatology nearly fifty years ago, neither of the main treatments Dr. Mangini uses had yet been invented. Isn't that correct?"

"I keep current with the standard of care in the field."

"And how do you do that, Dr. Baldwin?" I was genuinely curious.

"By reading medical journals, among other things."

"What 'other things,' may I ask? Do you attend trainings?" I received no answer from Baldwin except a simmering glare. "Do you take classes? Do you spend time on hospital units?"

"How *dare* you question my medical knowledge?" he exploded. "You're not a doctor!" His anger was coming out. Good. Maybe I could get it to play into my hands.

"I can see that it makes you very upset when someone questions your credentials," I said.

"You're damn right it does. I went through four years of medical school, another five years of residency and fellowship training, and, after that, twenty-five years of practice to earn my expertise!"

"So it must have galled you when Dr. Mangini began questioning your ability to judge the medical necessity of her procedures."

"It was not her place to impugn me!"

At this, Baldwin actually stood up and stormed out of the room. Clearly, he was personally incensed at Dr. M. I hoped this would show the jury that he had a strong motivation for retaliation.

He finally returned to the room in a calmer state.

A technique I sometimes try to use when deposing a witness is to ask questions in a leading form, so the witness thinks I already know the answers. Then I'll ask a question I *don't* know the answer to, in hopes that the witness will assume I already have that answer as well. It's Litigation 101, but sometimes, it works.

In this case, I asked Baldwin a series of leading questions in the vein of: *You worked for Employer x for y years, isn't that correct? And then you joined Omega in* year x, *isn't that right. And you're paid a fee for each claim you review, rather than a set salary, isn't that correct?* He gave me the repeated yeses I was expecting.

In addition, you receive a bonus at the end of each year, correct? Yes. *And that bonus is based on the amount of cost-savings Omega realizes from denying care that is not medically necessary, correct?*

I'd caught him off guard, but not enough to trip him up. He was smart enough to answer no to this question, but I could see suspicion in his eyes. He claimed not to know how his bonus was calculated. But his evasiveness convinced me that he *was* financially incentivized to deny claims. He viewed Tina as a threat not only to his ego but also to his wallet.

49

Each time Dr. M received a claim denial, she appealed it. And then the appeal went through virtually the identical process as the original review. The only difference was that the appeal was heard by a different medical director.

I was able to learn that, as with the initial claims reviews, Dr. M's appeals were assigned in a far-from-random way. There was only *one* doctor who reviewed all of Dr. M's appeals: a Dr. Valcourt. Valcourt had been inundated with appeals from Tina because, as I mentioned, Tina appealed each and every denied claim.

It was obvious, both from my deposition of Valcourt and from the timing of his actions, that he regarded Dr. M as a troublemaker. He reportedly told coworkers that Tina "wasn't following the rules"—that is, Omega's rules.

And Valcourt didn't like troublemakers. So he recommended Dr. M be placed on prepayment review (PPR), which meant that *all* of her claims would be flagged for review. It also meant that when Dr. M's claims were rejected (which was almost 100 percent of the time), letters would go out to Tina's patients stating that the services she had provided were "not medically necessary."

During my deposition of Valcourt, I figured it would be tricky to make him admit that he had put Dr. M on PPR as a punitive measure, but he surprised me. He seemed oddly intent on letting me know how powerful he was and how Omega held all the cards.

"It's important," he said, "that these doctors understand that, when it comes to coverage and payment decisions, *we* are in charge, not them."

"Are you aware of how physicians' lives and practices are affected when they are placed on PPR?" I asked him.

"Yes," he said unapologetically. "It can be financially devastating. I know that. Fewer of their claims are paid, and those that *are* paid take much longer. The doctor's reputation suffers. But that's the price they pay for not playing by the rules."

"So when you put someone on PPR, it's not strictly a medical decision; it's a punitive measure as well, right?"

Without hesitation, he replied, "Yes."

Wow—I couldn't believe my ears. This felt like that moment in *A Few Good Men* when the general, played by Jack Nicholson, admits to ordering a "code red." An Omega employee had just made a sworn admission that he had taken actions against Dr. M that were intended to be punitive.

Why was that significant? Well, there's a statute in California that protects physicians from exactly such treatment:

> No person or entity shall terminate, retaliate, or otherwise penalize a physician and surgeon for advocating for medically appropriate health care.

That law further states that "advocating for medically appropriate health care" includes "appeal[ing] a payer's decision to deny payment for a service"—exactly what Dr. M had been doing. Filing appeals, as was her ethical duty.

When I asked Valcourt for the "official" reason why Omega had terminated Dr. M, however, he knew better than to say, "To punish her sorry ass."

He replied, "Because we learned from the California Department of Insurance that Dr. Mangini was being investigated."

Tina, under investigation? Uh-oh. This was news to me.

"For what?" I asked.

"You'll have to ask the CDI," he responded.

50

So Omega was finally offering an actual reason for terminating Tina. This was starting to get interesting.

As I mentioned before, Omega stated in its termination letter to Dr. M that it was "terminating [her] contract effective in sixty days." No reason was given. When I propounded interrogatories about this, Omega responded, under oath: "Termination was without cause"—again, no reason. That was their story, and they were sticking to it.

But as often happens in these cases, as I began to assemble evidence of illegal and retaliatory behavior on the part of Omega, suddenly Omega changed its tune. It started to "remember" why it "really" terminated the doctor and to retroactively construct its own justification for the firing.

As discovery progressed, Omega started to disclose—through witnesses' depositions and in briefs to the court—that it was planning to put forth three main reasons why Dr. M was terminated: 1) the investigation by the CDI, 2) Tina's violation of billing and "other" insurer policies, and 3) a "lack of network need"—meaning Omega had a surplus of doctors in Tina's specialty and no longer needed her.

My gut sense was that they were building a house of cards. I would have to find a way to blow it down.

The first thing I needed to do was track this supposed investigation by the CDI (California Department of Insurance) to its origins. I went to work on that, and it took many months before I discovered the answer. Someone, it turned out, had indeed reported to the CDI that Dr. M was engaged in possible billing fraud.

But who had made these charges?

By digging deeper and reviewing literally hundreds of pages of e-mail strings, I finally found the answer—which I don't think Omega was even aware it had sent to me, so deeply was it buried in piles of correspondence. *Omega itself* was the entity that had reported Dr. M! The investigation had been closed by the CDI without any finding of fraud or misconduct. But now Omega was using its own self-originated and groundless allegation of billing fraud as its reason for terminating Dr. M!

Talk about circular reasoning.

As for Omega's claim that Tina had violated its policies, Omega could produce no specific charges nor any evidence to support concrete misbehavior on Tina's part. What *was* evident, at least to my eyes, was that Omega simply considered Dr. M a pain in the rear because of her relentless appeals of their decisions. And they wanted to get rid of her.

Finally, Omega's claim of "no network need" led to my uncovering yet another sleazy behavior on the part of the insurer, one I have found to be common in the insurance industry. Omega was claiming that it had terminated Dr. M in part because it had "no network need" for a doctor with Tina's specialty. When I requested evidence as to how this determination had been made, Omega couldn't produce it. Perhaps because it didn't exist.

As we were approaching the trial date, I went on Omega's website and opened the online version of its Provider Finder directory to see how many physicians with Dr. M's specialty were currently listed as in-network. I couldn't believe my eyes. There was Dr. Mangini's name, listed as an in-network provider. I had my client's office call Omega anonymously to find out if Dr. M was actually still in-network. "No," replied the insurer. But Omega was still using her name to advertise how many doctors it had in its provider network.

This continued listing of Dr. M as an Omega-approved doctor amounted, in my opinion, to fraudulent advertising. It also created more bad blood for Tina. Patients would find her name in the Provider Finder directory, come to see her, and learn only later that she was not in-network. Thus, Omega would refuse to pay their claims.

This is a rampant practice in the health insurance business, by the way. If you've ever tried to find an in-network physician for yourself, you may have had some experience with this. You see a doctor listed in the insurer's online directory, so you call his or her practice to make an appointment, only to learn that the practice doesn't actually accept your insurance. You try a second doctor, and then a third. Same story. You wonder how the insurer could be so inaccurate with its online directory. You chalk it up to sloppiness.

An aside from the Author: It's "deliberate sloppiness," in my opinion. Many of these insurers actually have small, narrow networks of physicians they work with, but they publish larger lists online, thereby creating the illusion that their provider network is much bigger than it is. If you make the mistake of calling one of these incorrectly listed doctors and making an appointment, you might find out only later that your insurance has not been accepted. The insurer is thus off the hook on paying. So it's to the insurer's advantage, in more ways than one, to "pad" its provider network directory.

I hoped I would have a chance to open the jury's eyes to this practice.

The trial date was now almost upon us, and it was time to run my case by my favorite test juror: my husband, Peter. We've been married for twenty-three years, and I always do a test presentation of my case for him to see whether it hangs together and makes compelling sense to

GREED ON TRIAL

a layperson. Peter's my biggest fan, but he always tells me honestly if there are gaps or muddy areas in my case. I laid out my arguments and my evidence proving that Dr. M was a conscientious doctor who went the extra mile for her patients, that she had been "flagged" for prejudicial treatment within the insurance company, that the medical directors who handled her claims had an ax to grind with her, that Omega's actions toward her had been punitive and retaliatory, that these actions had defamed Tina and caused her harm, and that the reasons Omega was offering for her termination were built on falsehoods and misdirection.

Peter smiled. "I think you've got this one, sweetie. I wish the defamation angle were a little stronger, but I think you've got it."

Damn. *I* wished my defamation case were a little stronger, too.

51

A final twist occurred before we stepped into the courtroom. Just a couple of weeks before trial was set to begin, I learned—from court filings submitted by the opposition—that Tina had had a complaint filed against her with the medical board. This had nothing to do with that empty CDI investigation that Omega had instigated; this was a separate issue entirely. And it was a more serious one.

Suddenly, I was facing every attorney's nightmare—your own client has withheld damaging information from you.

"Why didn't you tell me about this?" I demanded of Tina.

"I didn't think it was important," she replied. "The charges are groundless, and I'm sure they're going to be dismissed."

"Regardless. They haven't been dismissed *yet*. And now Omega's lawyers know about them. I wish you had told me about this."

"It has nothing to do with this case, though."

"Are you absolutely sure about that?"

Tina didn't answer.

Medical board proceedings are confidential, so I had to conduct my own legal discovery process to find out who had reported Dr. M and why. It turned out that the complaint had been filed by a patient of Dr. M.

Uh-oh. My heart plunged into my belly. Regardless of how serious the charges were or were not, I knew the defense was going to have a field day with this.

I went home, had a glass of wine (OK, maybe two), and stewed in my frustration. "Clients don't understand the position they put their attorneys in when they omit crucial facts," I complained to Peter. "Tina has shot herself in the foot by playing doctor with the truth." Peter and I watched a movie on HBO, and I tried to put the case out of my mind. No joy. Finally, I opted for a cheesy novel and an early bedtime.

I dozed for maybe an hour or two before my mind jerked me from sleep. I don't typically get a lot of sleep in the weeks approaching trial. I'm always sure there's some crucial fact I've overlooked, and I have a habit of scanning my memory banks in the wee hours of the night, trying to identify that one detail I've forgotten. I have tried meditating, I've tried reading boring books, I've even tried melatonin, but nothing works; I can't seem to shut my brain off when a trial is approaching. At two in the morning I'm always certain I'm going to lose.

In this case, I knew exactly what I was worried about. That damned patient complaint against Tina. *What do we know about the patient who filed it?* I asked myself. Not much, I realized. I went down the hallway and opened up my trial box. I discovered that the woman had her insurance through Omega. The reason she'd filed the complaint, it seemed, was that she had received one of those infamous denial letters stating, "The services you received from Dr. Mangini were not medically necessary." As a result, she quite understandably thought Dr. M had performed unnecessary procedures on her. And, in turn, she filed a complaint.

Wait a minute, I realized. *This letter might be the key.*

In the morning, I called Tina and asked to meet with her again.

"Omega's lawyers are going to use this medical board complaint against you in court," I told her.

"Is there anything we can do to fight them on that?" Tina pleaded. "I don't want this stuff coming out. My reputation has suffered enough already."

"We *could* file a motion to suppress."

"Yes, that sounds good, let's do that."

"I'm sure that's exactly what Omega's expecting us to do," I replied. "But know what I think?"

Tina waited expectantly.

"I think we should do the opposite. I think we should surprise them. I want to put you on the witness stand and question you about this medical board complaint."

"What? Are you crazy? Why would you do that?"

"Think about it, Tina. We're trying to convince the jury that Omega's actions—in particular, sending those 'not medically necessary' letters to your patients—were defamatory and injurious to you, right?"

"Right."

"So what better way to prove that than with actual evidence? One of your patients *filed a complaint with the medical board* as a direct result of receiving one of those letters from Omega."

Tina nodded, taking in what I was saying but still not sure where I was headed.

"Getting investigated by the medical board is serious business, isn't it?" I asked her.

"Absolutely," said Tina. "It can be extremely damaging to your reputation. You can even end up losing your license to practice."

"So what Omega did to you was directly injurious. Don't you see?"

Light was dawning on Tina's face.

"In most of my cases," I continued, "it's hard to prove concretely that the insurer's denial letters actually caused the client harm. Here, we can prove it in dramatic fashion: Patient receives letter from Omega stating your procedure was unnecessary. Patient goes to medical board and files complaint against you. Medical board launches investigation. And now *Omega itself* is trying to use the very fact of that investigation to damage your reputation, in real time, right in front of a jury. It doesn't get any better than that."

Tina smiled and said, "Bring it on."

PART VI

A Dermatologist's Tale

The Trial

52

We're a week and a half into the trial when I find myself sitting in the witness room off the courtroom, face to face with the defense team. We're waiting for the final member of the defense team to arrive. The jury has been sent home for the day, and it's just us lawyers. Something unusual has happened in this case. Right after I finished cross-examining one of the defense witnesses—a cross-examination that produced some surprising and explosive testimony—the defense attorney, Jim Stoppard, shot me a look of surrender and said, "I think it's time for us to chat."

Now the defense wants to talk settlement. So here we are.

Settlements are not unusual. In fact, the great majority of my cases are resolved this way. What's unusual here is the timing of the settlement. Quite often, a case will settle before it ever sees the inside of a courtroom. Also quite often, as I explained earlier, a case will settle once the defense learns there are going to be punitive damages. But it's rare that the defense will move to fold its cards in the middle of a trial. (It does happen, though. I've seen settlements occur at some very odd moments.) It usually signifies that something has gone pretty dramatically wrong for the defense.

In this case, it wasn't just one thing; it was everything—though the testimony of Wanda Sampson, the Omega employee in charge of PPR, was the final straw. I'd love to take all the credit for the defense's collapse, but, in truth, this was just one of those cases that was born under a black cloud. They happen from time to time. The defense was on the receiving end of it this time, but I've been there, and it isn't fun.

Looking back on the way the trial unfolded, things started to go wonky for the defense before the first witness was even called . . .

At the beginning of voir dire, Judge Jules Ramirez was explaining to the jury who the two parties in the trial were. "The defendant in this case is Omega Health, the large insurance company," she said, "and the plaintiff is Dr. Tina Mangini. She has alleged that Omega terminated her from their provider network in a retaliatory and damaging manner. Now, I'm sure most or all of you have heard of Omega Health. It's a well-known company that advertises on television, the radio, billboards, and magazines. So who here has had some direct experience with this company?"

Many hands went up, and one juror mistakenly thought he had been given permission to speak. Before Attorney Stoppard or the judge could stop him, he blurted out, "I get my insurance through these guys, and they're terrible. I've got a liver condition, but they deny every claim I put in. Then they deny my appeals, too. Deny, deny, deny, that's all these clowns do. They're all about the red tape." The judge finally stopped the man and dismissed him from the jury pool, but now the whole panel had heard his rant against Omega. This could definitely be characterized as prejudicial. (Having dealt with Omega myself, I didn't feel a lot of sympathy for them, but I did feel bad for their attorneys.)

The defense immediately requested a sidebar with the judge. We went into chambers, and Stoppard moved for a mistrial. I would have done the same had I been in his shoes. Judge Ramirez was reluctant to declare a mistrial. Judges always are. They don't want to lose all the time the court has already invested in the case, and they want to keep things moving. So Judge Ramirez denied the motion. This was good news for us. (But it came with an asterisk. Now the defense had grounds for appeal.)

So the defense had been staggered by a PR blow before testimony even started. The next big thing that went sideways for them was when they tried to "catch" Tina on the medical board complaint. Dr. M and I had ultimately agreed that we would not introduce this issue ourselves, as I had originally proposed. However, we would be very prepared to face it head on in the event the defense brought it up on cross. Stoppard wasn't expecting us to be so prepared. He thought he had a "gotcha."

"You testified, did you not," said Stoppard to Dr. M, who was sitting on the witness stand, "that you had never been in trouble or faced any sort of discipline as a doctor?"

"That's correct," replied Tina.

Stoppard turned to the audience, raising his eyebrows theatrically, then turned back toward Tina. "But that's not really true, is it? Weren't you recently under investigation by the medical board?"

The jury reacted in obvious surprise to this one. Stoppard had his "Perry Mason" moment. Or so he thought.

Stoppard proceeded to present documents showing that Tina was indeed under investigation for performing procedures that were deemed medically unnecessary.

"Do you recognize this letter from the medical board?" Stoppard asked.

"Yes," said Dr. M.

"And what does it say?"

"It's informing me that I'm under investigation."

"So it's not true, is it, that you've never been in any sort of trouble?"

"Technically, no," said Dr. M. "But that investigation is—"

"Nothing further," said Stoppard, cutting my client off.

Stoppard wrapped up his cross-examination at this point, looking pretty confident.

I was now allowed to do a "redirect" examination in order to challenge anything that had come up on cross.

During my redirect, I revealed, through questioning my witness and through introducing further documents, that the investigation in question had been prompted by—as I explained earlier—a complaint from one of Tina's patients to the medical board. I'm able to show that the patient received a letter stating that a procedure Dr. M had performed on her was medically unnecessary—and that this was why she'd filed a complaint with the board.

When I displayed the letter for the court, it became dramatically clear from the letterhead and the signature that the decision of medical nonnecessity had been made by a medical director who *worked for the defendant.*

In other words, *the defendant itself had made the decision that prompted the patient to file the complaint. This nonnecessity decision was part of the defendant's overall pattern of denying treatments to patients, which was one of the very problems my client took issue with!*

"Do you agree with the medical director's decision that your treatment of this patient was not medically necessary?" I asked Tina on the stand.

"I most definitely do not. And I appealed that decision vigorously, furnishing Omega with a great deal of evidence to support my position, including photographs and descriptions of best practices."

"And what was the defendant's response?"

"I received a form rejection letter, the same one they sent me for probably fifty other appeals."

"Nothing further, Your Honor."

The defense's circularity had been unmasked, and I thought Stoppard looked much worse for having brought the whole issue up—not only because Omega was shown to have triggered the board complaint against Tina *and* damaged her in the process but also because we were able to point out to the jury Omega's habit of rejecting valid medical claims and appeals.

From the look on Stoppard's face, he knew he had stepped in something he wished he'd walked around.

53

The next critical juncture of the trial involved an Omega Health medical director. Again, luck played a role in how this witness's testimony unfolded.

"Medical directors" are crucial players within insurance companies and health-care systems. Their job is to make decisions about the medical necessity of procedures and to review appeals of those decisions. Also, when a physician needs to be brought in line and coaxed into playing ball, it's often medical directors who perform this task.

I have a bit of an issue with medical directors, I'll admit. That's because I believe they are used somewhat dishonestly by "the system". On paper, they look like working doctors—a *higher level* of working doctor, in fact, because they have presumably *earned* the title "director." But this isn't a hospital-type situation, where the heads of departments *really are* the more skilled and experienced physicians. Many "medical directors," in fact, haven't treated an actual patient in years or even decades. They handle paperwork only. Many of them have business degrees alongside their MDs because they've been on an administrative track the bulk of their careers. But, again, on paper they appear to be high-level physicians. Part of my trial strategy often involves exposing this illusion to juries.

"The plaintiff may call its next witness," said Judge Ramirez.

"We call Dr. Emil Valcourt."

After Valcourt was sworn in, I kicked things off by asking him, "Who is your employer?"

"It *was* the defendant. I'm now on disability."

"And when did you start on disability?"

"March 16."

"So just ten days ago?"

"Yes."

The timing of his disability retirement seemed highly suspicious, and I wanted to bring that out to the jury. Valcourt had left his job just ten days before trial started—and I'd had to hire a private eye to track him down.

"What was your role at Omega Health?"

"I was a medical director."

"And what were your qualifications to perform this role?"

"I have an MD from Temple University."

"But it appears from your records that you also have an MBA from business school and a JD degree from law school."

"That's correct."

"That's a lot of schooling."

"It is indeed."

"Not a lot of time for practicing medicine."

"Objection"—Stoppard.

"Sustained"—Judge Ramirez.

I soldiered on. "And who was your employer before you worked at Omega?" I asked him.

"I worked for Pacific Health Partners for five years."

"And before that?"

We verbally tracked his employment back through the years, and I was able to establish that he had been working for a series of insurance companies and health plans going back two decades.

"Have you *ever* taken care of real, live patients, Dr. Valcourt?"

"Yes, I did, for several years," he said with some pride.

"If I'm reading your employment history correctly, it's been twenty-three years since you last treated a patient. Isn't that correct?"

"I'll take your word for the math," said Valcourt.

"And what was your specialty when you *did* treat patients all those many years ago?"

"I was an ob–gyn."

"I see. Not dermatology. Why aren't you still practicing?"

"Because, frankly, I didn't like waking up at three in the morning to deliver babies." Polite laughter from the jury box.

"So working with real patients was pretty tough, eh? Is it fair to say, based on your employment history and your educational choices, that you have been preparing most of your life to be a medical *director*, not a practicing physician?"

"I'm proud of what I've done with my career."

"That's not what I asked, but I think you've answered my question. So let's talk about some of your job responsibilities as medical director." Through a series of questions, I established that his job was twofold. First, he had to review appeals of medical necessity decisions. Second, he had to recommend when and if a physician should be placed on PPR and/or ultimately terminated from Omega's provider network.

"When you denied treatments to patients as 'not medically necessary,'" I said, "the decision was based on paper records only, isn't that right? You did not see actual patients, did you?"

"Not as a rule."

"So there were occasional times you *did* see a live patient?"

He grumbled and shifted in his seat. "No."

"Did you talk to the treating physicians when making these decisions about medical necessity?"

"That was not the normal protocol we followed, no." Valcourt was growing steadily testier.

"And you reviewed cases of neurologists, orthopedic surgeons, oncologists, and many other specialists, is that right?"

"Yes."

"Even though your own training and experience—which came to an end twenty-three years ago—was only in obstetrics and gynecology?"

This time, Valcourt just glared at me.

"Answer the question, please," instructed the judge.

"Yes, I reviewed cases involving many medical specialties."

"Did you ever receive appeals from my client?"

"No."

Aha. I had "innocently" dropped this question in as part of my general background questioning, but he had now testified that he had not received any appeals from Dr. M, which I knew was not true. This was something I could use.

"Now, as part of your job, did you also do so-called 'meet-and-confers' with doctors?"

"Yes," he replied.

"These are face-to-face meetings that occur between doctors and medical directors if the doctor believes his or her appeals have been wrongfully denied."

"Correct."

"And did you ever engage in a meet-and-confer with my client?" This was a crucial question, since Stoppard had claimed in his opening statement that no one from the defendant company had ever met my client.

"I don't recall."

"Why is that? Because you do so many of these meet-and-confers?"

This question put him in a tricky position. If he said yes, that would indicate that the company routinely denied large numbers of appeals from doctors. If he said no, it would look suspicious that he didn't remember my client. He squirmed in silence as he tried to frame an answer. Sensing his discomfort, I tossed him an unplanned question, just to see how he'd react. "You *are* aware why we're here in court, are you not, Dr. Valcourt?"

"Yes," he blurted out. "Because the doctor is not happy about being terminated by our company!"

Wow. He had just said it. *Terminated.* The word the defense had been studiously trying to avoid had just slipped out of his mouth. Triggered by a lucky question.

54

"Were you involved in the decision to *terminate* my client?" I asked Valcourt, using the word he himself had just used.

"Yes, that was one of my duties as medical director," he replied.

"Was anyone else involved in that decision to terminate?" I asked, hitting that word again.

"Yes, some other medical directors and members of the management team were involved," he replied.

"And what was the reason for the termination of my client?"

"It was a business decision."

Hmm, where have I heard that line before? I thought to myself. *(Answer: in half the cases I've tried.)*

"And in your experience, Dr. Valcourt, do insurance companies typically make business decisions for no reason?"

"No." Annoyance beamed from his eyes.

"Then what was the reason you decided to terminate my client?"

He didn't want to answer, but he had to say something, or he would look foolish.

"There was no network need for her services."

"By that, do you mean Omega already had enough doctors with the same specialty as my client?"

"That's correct."

"And when was my client told that lack of network need was the reason for her termination?"

"I don't know."

"Who told the doctor that?"

"I don't know."

"How was the doctor told that?"

"I don't know."

"*Was* the doctor told that?"

"I don't know."

Stoppard stared at Valcourt in disbelief from the defense table. Clearly, he was expecting better answers from this defense-friendly witness. So was I, truth be told.

"How many other doctors of the same specialty were in the network at the time my client was terminated?" I continued.

"I don't recall."

"What information about network need did you and the other decision makers refer to so that you could make such a decision?"

"I don't recall."

"Determining network need is part of your job, but you don't recall what criteria, if any, you used?"

Valcourt didn't answer. I let his silence ferment.

"Isn't it true, Dr. Valcourt, that the real reason for my client's termination was that my client advocated for her patients by repeatedly appealing denied claims?"

"No, that's not the reason," Valcourt said, folding his arms in protest.

"Ah, finally something you *do* know. You do admit that this doctor was a strong advocate for patients, though, do you not?"

"I don't know."

"Ah, back to 'I don't know.' I'll put it more specifically. You *do* know that this doctor appealed many denied treatment decisions, do you not?"

"No, I don't know that."

"Let me clarify your answer: Are you saying that the doctor did not appeal claims, or that *you* don't know?"

"I'm saying that *I* don't know."

"Well, you actually received many, many appeals from my client and responded to them, did you not?"

"Not that I recall."

Ah, here it was: my "in"! "I want to be extremely clear about this, Dr. Valcourt. Did you *not receive appeals* from my client, or do you just *not recall* whether you received them?"

"I don't recall."

"Because earlier, when I asked, 'Did you ever receive appeals from my client?' you answered no."

A "deer in the headlights" look came over his face for a moment. Several of the jurors leaned forward in their seats. I let the moment ripen.

"I don't like to call people liars, Dr. Valcourt," I said. And that was true; I don't. "So which answer do you want to pick: You did not receive appeals from the doctor, or you do not recall?"

At last, his defiance bubbled over. "I did not receive such appeals!"

I showed Valcourt a large collection of response letters to Tina, signed by Valcourt himself. "Can you look at exhibits F through Y? Are these, or are they not, letters from you to the doctor, rejecting her appeals?"

"I don't recall these, but I do not deny they have my electronic signature."

"So you don't recall sending these letters to my client?"

"Not specifically, no."

"There are twenty of them here, dated over a two-year period of time. You don't recall sending *any* of them?"

"No."

He was looking really bad to the jury at this point. His credibility was utterly shot.

"Not one? Do you recall meeting in person with my client?"

"No."

I showed him notes from a meet-and-confer taken by his own company's in-house attorney, Stephanie Atwood, who was present in court and had also been present at the meet-and-confer. The notes listed Valcourt as a participant.

"Still having trouble with your memory?" I prodded him. "If so, maybe Ms. Atwood can help you. Were you at this meeting, where my client presented several of her patients' cases?"

"Yes! I was at the meeting!"

"There, that wasn't so hard now, was it? So you *did* meet my client, then. And was my client advocating for patients at this meeting?"

"That's the purpose of the meet-and-confer."

"So I'll ask this one more time. The fact that my client advocated so strongly for patients—that was the real reason you terminated my client, wasn't it?"

"No."

His no rings hollow, though. I'm pretty sure the jury has already made up its mind about the good doctor Valcourt. And I'm pretty sure Stoppard knows it.

"I have nothing more for this witness, Your Honor."

55

A court officer comes into the witness room and brings us all bottled water. We're still waiting for the final member of the defense team to join us for the settlement meeting, so I have time to reflect some more on the events that brought us to this place.

The next important development in the trial stemmed from a strategic error that I made. It put a temporary kink in my case, but ultimately, I think it did permanent damage to the defense . . .

I wanted to reveal the whole "no network need" thing as a sham, so I called the VP in charge of physician contracting, Sheila Owens, to the stand.

I already knew from the flimsy evidence that had been furnished to me during discovery that the defense had little to back up its claim that "lack of network need" was the real reason for my client's dismissal. The only evidence that had been offered was an alleged printout of an online search of Omega's provider directory. The printout showed that there were 137 doctors with my client's specialty within ten miles of the search location.

The first thing I asked Owens was, "Do you claim it was your job to do the analysis of network need for this doctor?" I phrased it this way on purpose; I wanted the jury to know I wasn't buying it. I didn't think *anyone* had analyzed network need in this case.

"Yes," Owens said, but she didn't make eye contact with me.

"So when did you do this supposed analysis?"

"I can't recall."

"Ah . . . Popular response these days."

I showed her the alleged search printout. "Did you do the online search that this printout supposedly represents?"

"Yes," said Owens.

"And how many pages is this document, which the defense placed into evidence?"

"One."

"Can you please read the words in the upper right corner?"

"It reads, 'Page one of two.'"

"So this is not the complete document, is it?"

"Evidently not," acknowledged Owens.

"How many doctors' names came up as the search result?"

"It says here, '137.'"

"I can see that. But page one, the only page we've been given, lists only seven names. So . . . what, there were 130 names on page two?"

"I don't know."

"According to this printout, there was only one doctor with my client's specialty in the same zip code as my client, isn't that right?"

"So it would appear."

"Does that make any sense, if, as you claim, there were 137 similar specialists within a ten-mile radius?"

"I don't know."

"When did you do this online search, Ms. Owens?"

"I can't recall exactly."

"And where is your name on this document?"

"I don't see it."

"And where is the name of the doctor, my client, on this document?"

"I don't see it."

"Can you swear with certainty that this particular search was even done in relation to this particular doctor?"

"It's difficult to tell from the document."

"It certainly is, isn't it? This document does not appear to prove anything at all, does it, Ms. Owen?"

"Not really."

"But I'm sure, as a specialist in these matters, you must use methods a lot more sophisticated than an online search tool when making your determinations of network need."

"Well, yes."

"Can you tell us how those determinations are made?

"We don't like to have more than a certain number of physicians of a given specialty within a given geographic radius."

"And what are the actual numbers you use?"

"I don't recall offhand. I believe we try to have no more than one specialist per fifteen hundred members."

"Now you're talking *member* numbers; you just said your determination was based on geographic area."

"Well, we . . . we . . . we use a number of different criteria," she said.

"So you use some kind of formula?"

"You could say that."

"So what *is* that formula?"

"It's not hard and fast. It varies on a case-by-case basis. There are a lot of factors involved."

"I see. So you can basically change the formula as you see fit—for example, if you don't like a certain doctor and you just want to get rid of them?"

"Objection."

"Sustained."

"How many doctors with my client's specialty are *currently* practicing within a twenty-five-mile radius of my client's former office?" I asked.

"I couldn't answer that with any kind of accuracy."

And here was where I made my big goof—I underestimated the deviousness of my opponent.

"Well, maybe we can answer that question *together* with some accuracy," I said. "Your Honor, I request permission to show the defendants' provider directory live on the overhead. We can go to the website and pull it up right now." I had looked at Omega's online directory just that morning, so I knew what the search would turn up.

"Objection!" The defense came hurrying to the bench after asking for a sidebar, and we ended up going into chambers. The defense attorneys didn't want me showing a live Web page to the jury until they'd viewed it themselves; they were afraid of being blindsided by something unexpected. I didn't blame them. I'd have been cautious in their position, too.

"But I'm allowed to show witnesses documents to refresh their recollection," I reminded the judge, "so what are the grounds for stopping me?"

"I'm ruling with the plaintiff on this one," the judge said to Stoppard, then turned to me. "You can show the website. I'm familiar with how a search is done, so I will talk your trial tech through the steps and authenticate the search as we go."

We were ready to roll with that plan, but when we came out of chambers, the judge looked at the clock. "It's 11:40," she said. "In the interest of efficiency, let's take our lunch break now, so the computer search can be set up and ready to roll without delay when we return." She told the jury what was going to happen, and then we recessed for lunch.

By the time I arrived at the lunchroom in the basement of the courthouse—I always eat my lunch at the same courthouse cafeteria where the jury eats—I could see my trial tech staring blankly at me as I crossed the floor.

"I would tell you you're not going to believe this," he said, "but I know you will. I'm on the Internet right now, and when I pull up Omega's provider directory, this is what I see." He angled his laptop toward me. The screen read, "This page is temporarily unavailable due to technical difficulties."

What? Really? These guys had a reputation for playing dirty, but I didn't think they'd stoop to this. My bad. Live and learn.

The website was "out of order" and remained so for the rest of the trial.

56

I learned a big lesson that day; I will never again "go live" on the Internet in a courtroom without taking careful precautions first.

I'd suffered a knockdown, no doubt. But then a subtle turning point took place in the trial. After lunch, as I explained to Judge Ramirez and the defense in chambers that the defendants' website had "mysteriously" stopped functioning, I saw something come over Ramirez's eyes. Her facial expression said that she knew exactly what the defendant had pulled and was extremely angry about it. But she also knew that she couldn't *prove* wrongdoing, not right then and there.

So she went out to the bench and made a neutral statement to the jury that there had been a change of ruling and we wouldn't be looking at the website after all.

But from the cold look Ramirez gave Stoppard as the proceedings continued, I knew she was simmering about it and that she had "turned against" the defense. Judges, of course, are supposed to remain neutral and unbiased throughout the trial, but judges are also human beings. And sometimes you can feel it: that moment in a trial when a judge flips internally toward one side or the other. I felt it in that moment, and I knew that we now had a proplaintiff judge sitting on the bench. I'm pretty sure Stoppard knew it too. I could tell by the sudden ring of dampness around his collar.

No sympathy from me, my friend. What goes around comes around.

The defense had submitted a medium-long witness list, but when it came time to present their case, they called only a few witnesses to the stand; I had the sense they were already feeling pretty defeated. Wanda Sampson was the final nail in their coffin.

As Stoppard stepped up to the stand to question Sampson, the first thing he did was establish that she was employed by the defendant.

"And what department do you work in, Ms. Sampson?"

"I run the prepayment review, or PPR, unit."

"Can you tell me what a PPR is?"

"Well, when a doctor has been flagged as 'problematic' in some way by one or more of the medical directors, they may be placed on PPR. This means, in short, that their billing practices are given an extra layer of review. *Everything* they submit is reviewed by our team before it is approved for payment."

"And why are doctors placed on PPR?"

"To improve patient care, of course."

Of course. "To improve patient care" was the blanket justification used to explain any questionable behavior on the part of insurers and health-care systems.

"And why was the plaintiff placed on PPR, do you recall?"

"The plaintiff was viewed by management as not a very good doctor."

"How do you mean?"

"Our profiling showed that this doctor did not practice like other doctors and was not providing efficient, quality care—"

"Objection," I said. Though I try, as a rule, to object as little as possible in court, I couldn't allow this witness to continue badmouthing my client. "This calls for expert testimony. This witness is not an expert on what constitutes good medical care."

"Sustained," said the judge, adding gently, "and please refrain from presenting an argument when you object, Ms. Barta."

"Yes, Your Honor."

When it was my turn to cross-examine this witness, I fired a couple of questions from my seat. "Being on PPR makes things very difficult for doctors, doesn't it, Ms. Sampson?"

"So I'm told."

"PPR is used as a form of punishment, isn't it?"

"That's your word; I wouldn't characterize it that way."

Next, I decided to do something that might seem crazy at first blush, but I did it for a couple of reasons. First, I wanted to shake up the jury a bit and make them pay attention—we were at that point in the trial where many of them start to glaze over. Second, I was setting a snare that I hoped the witness would step into.

I patted Dr. M's arm and whispered, "Don't worry." And then I stepped up to the witness and said, "Isn't the real reason you placed my client on PPR because there had been reports to the California Department of Insurance about my client engaging in billing fraud?" As you may recall, this was that second complaint that had been filed against my client—not the medical board complaint but a separate issue.

I saw the eyes of several jurors go wide: *Why is she throwing her client under the bus like this?* The witness, too, looked surprised, and I could tell she was wondering what I was up to. Then I saw the decision-making process play out on her face. *Well, if the plaintiff's own attorney is going to hand me a gift, I'm damn well going to take it.*

"As a matter of fact, yes, that *was* a major reason the doctor was placed on PPR. We were concerned about possible billing fraud."

I displayed some e-mails I had gathered in discovery. First, I highlighted a name on one of them.

"Do you recognize this name, Ms. Sampson?"

"Alberta Merlini. Yes, she works for our company, Omega Health."

I then brought up another e-mail. "This e-mail reveals who filed the report with the CDI. Can you read me the name of the person who filed it, please?"

"Alberta Merlini," read the witness, her voice flat.

"So what happened here, essentially, is that an Omega employee filed a report with the CDI, and then Omega used the fact that a report had been filed as a justification for placing my client on PPR. Isn't that right?" This was another instance of Omega using deceitful, circular reasoning to damage my client. Only this instance was even more egregious and deliberate than the last.

At this point, the witness's mouth went up and down in a very respectable imitation of a goldfish on a rug. Before she could even reply, I pressed on. "Isn't the real reason my client was placed on PPR because she was seen as a problem?"

"Yes, that's right!" she replied, startling me—and the rest of the courtroom—with the fervor of her tone. She stared at me in defiant anger. "She was an outlier."

"And by outlier, do you mean that this doctor was doing something different than the other doctors?"

"Yes, she certainly was!"

"She was doing things like making phone calls to your office appealing decisions by Omega medical director's that went against optimal patient care?"

"This doctor was *flaunting the guidelines!*"

"Going against the rules?"

"Absolutely!"

"Whose rules?" I pushed her.

"Ours, of course!" she declared as if issuing a royal decree. She actually rose out of her seat as she said this.

"And something needed to be done," I said. "She needed to be punished?"

"You're darn right she did! Rules need to be enforced, or they have no meaning!" Amazing. Just as Dr. Valcourt had done during depositions, she had pulled a Jack Nicholson, admitting to a code red. She had admitted to using PPR punitively. Again, I wish I could attribute her admission to my skill as an attorney, but it was almost as if she had this stuff stored up inside her and was just looking for an excuse to release it.

"No further questions of this witness."

I headed back to the plaintiffs' table. And it was at that moment that Stoppard quietly said to me, "Maybe it's time we had a chat."

57

So here we are in the witness room. The final member of the defense team bustles in, apologizing for her lateness, and sits. We all look at one another across the table.

It is obvious, without anyone needing to explain it, that the defendant recognizes that it's in a jam. Money isn't really the big issue for the defendant, and we all know it. The defendant is worried about what the jury will decide and is willing to pay liberally in order to avoid the bad publicity of a negative verdict. So I ask for X million dollars. It's on the high side, and we all know it, but not outlandishly so. Stoppard doesn't flinch. In fact, he would write us a check right there on the spot if he had Omega's checkbook.

But, of course, Omega wants concessions in exchange for its settlement. They want the verdict kept confidential—that means no disclosures to *anyone* about the amount *and* no press conference or statements of any kind to the media. The press has been following this case, and there are members of the press waiting down the hall as we speak. If I agree to this confidentiality, I won't be allowed to say a word to them.

Confidentiality, FYI, is a standard request in almost all settlements. It may seem like a small price to pay, but it's really not. Because it means that now no one will know that a doctor sued Omega and won. It means Big Insurance continues to look unassailable. But it's a price I usually have to agree to. It's typically nonnegotiable.

In this case, though, I want something more in return. The defense knows it's in trouble, and it also knows the press is waiting down the hall. So I make an additional demand: my client will agree to the confidentiality if Omega agrees to put her back in the provider network. The defense accepts this demand without hesitation.

When Tina learns that she's back on the insurance rolls, she releases the most profound sigh of relief I have ever heard. All she ever really wanted was to practice medicine in good conscience, without fear of reprisal. And now she can do that. She is happy, and that means I am happy.

People sometimes ask me, "If it's obvious you're going to win a case, what's your motivation, as the plaintiff, for settling?" It's a good question, given the fact that juries tend to be generous when it comes to punitive damages.

I have a few reasons. The first is that, believe it or not, I'm not actually greedy, and neither are most of my clients. My clients, as a rule, are good, compassionate people who became doctors for a reason. They're not vindictive by nature. Neither they nor I want to put anyone out of business. We don't want to see hundreds of doctors, or others, out of work or thousands of patients scrambling for new health care or insurance. I have actually been in a situation where I've known the jury was prepared to award damages so large they were going to bankrupt the defendant—and that's not good for anyone.

Another reason why I usually settle is that settling gives the client a chance to put the whole thing to rest, once and for all. Settling means there won't be any appeals by the other side—and appeals can sometimes drag on for three to five years or longer. That's not good for anyone but the lawyers. Settling means life can go on—the client can return to a normal life and normal practice.

The main reward, though, is seeing my clients' self-esteem and dignity restored. They are finally able to step out from under the cloud of suspicion they've been under since they were fired or terminated. They are able to feel some vindication and even receive some admiration and praise for having done the right thing and gone after Goliath. They are able to hold their heads high and tell their children and grandchildren to fight for what is right. They are made whole financially. And they're able to resume their place as fully respected and honored members of the medical community—which is all they ever wanted in the first place.

And what do I, personally, get out of all this, besides a nice fee and a "job well done"? Well . . .

As we're walking out of the settlement meeting, Tina turns to me, wearing an inner glow I haven't seen on her since this whole mess started, and says, "John and I are going to the lake this weekend. Any chance you and Peter can join us as our guests?"

"We'd love to."

. . . I get a friendship for life. And you can't put a price tag on that.

PART VII

A Neurologist's Tale

Doctor and Patient

58

Something about Caroline's dad seemed *off* to her. It had been a couple of months since she'd last seen him, and today he seemed oddly . . . diminished. Maybe it was the way his body stooped as he ambled over to give her a hug. Maybe it was the thin, reedy voice with which he said, "Hello, sweetie, so good to see you." Mike Rennan was in his mid-sixties—perhaps not a young, or even a middle-aged, man anymore, but too young to be losing the spring in his step. Maybe he was just tired or "off his game" today, but Caroline's inner sensors were firing. The silent concern in her mother's eyes did nothing to alleviate her worry.

Caroline usually visited her parents at least a couple of times a month, on weekends. She lived less than five miles away. But recently, some things had come up in her personal and work schedules, and two months had slipped by. The changes in her dad weren't *huge*, and she might not even have noticed them if she had been seeing him every two weeks, but the two-month gap brought them into sharp relief.

"How are you feeling, Dad? Everything OK?"

"Still having that damn problem with my hand, but other than that, all systems are go."

Caroline's dad had complained to his wife, Marie, recently that his hand was cramping up and shaking when he tried to write, which is not a small thing when you're a writer. And Mike Rennan was old school; he did his writing longhand, on yellow legal pads, and then typed it into a computer later for editing and polishing. Mike had had a long and successful career as a screenwriter and producer in Hollywood. Always an active man, he was beginning to slow down a bit work-wise—by choice—but he was still in the game. He was working on a new screenplay and did a fair amount of consulting in the movie business. His expertise was still in demand.

Caroline wandered into his office and looked at his desk. There they were, as expected: the stacks of yellow legal pads, one stack for each project, each pad folded open to the current page. Those yellow pads had been a staple of her childhood. Mike would leave them all over the house. The loose, free-flowing scrawl on those remembered yellow pages was so familiar to her, she felt she knew her dad's handwriting even better than she knew her own.

That was why she was so alarmed when she picked up one of the pads.

Mike's handwriting had changed, dramatically. It had become small, cramped, dark. It looked, in fact, as if a new person had been writing in Dad's pads. The changes in his handwriting plus the fact that Dad didn't even seem to be aware of them were setting off alarms in Caroline in a way that even the changes in his gait and his voice had not. Those bodily changes were subjective and might have been the result of Dad being a little under the weather. But the changes in his writing were concrete, measurable. She felt as if she were looking at documentation of some sort of deterioration.

"Dad, I think you should see a doctor. I'm seeing some things that have me a little worried."

"I'm fine. I don't need any doctors poking around in my skull and sending me bills."

"I've been trying to get him to see a doctor for months now," said Marie, Caroline's mom. "He refuses to go."

"What if *I* call and make an appointment with a neurologist?" asked Caroline. "Will you go then?"

Mike Rennan shrugged. Caroline knew her dad wouldn't want to be rude or unappreciative toward his daughter. She took his noncommittal shrug as a green light.

Of course, Caroline should have known better than to think she could just pick up the phone and make an appointment with a specialist in today's brave new medical world. Mike Rennan's medical plan was with a large health-care system called Coral Health. His plan allowed him to see any of the doctors "employed by any of the medical groups" that were part of the system, but if he wanted to see a specialist, he'd have to get a referral.

Translation: Mike would need to see a primary care physician first. After that, if (and only if) the PCP thought he should see a neurologist, he would be referred to one.

She called Triton Medical Group and was given an appointment one month away. She protested and asked for a sooner date, but was told this was the best they could do.

Caroline's gut was telling her a month might be too long.

59

Caroline and her mom accompanied Mike to the appointment. Caroline couldn't help noticing the stiff way her dad's arms hung at his side as he walked into Triton's clinic. They didn't seem to swing in a natural way anymore.

The Rennans were shown to an exam room. After they talked their way through the parade of medical assistants asking questions and typing data into computer screens, Dr. Rachel Polcyk, a PCP at the medical group, entered the room. She flashed a quick smile at them and asked why they were here.

"So that my father can get a referral to a specialist," said Caroline.

Caroline thought she saw Dr. Polcyk tense up ever so slightly, as if some subtle territorial line had been crossed. "We don't automatically 'give referrals,'" the PCP explained to the family. "I'll examine your dad, and if there is reason for further concern, or if I see anything we can't handle here, we'll talk about a referral."

"I didn't mean to suggest . . ." Caroline stopped herself before she said anything else she might regret.

Dr. Polcyk gave Mike what Caroline considered a cursory physical exam—a quick look in his eyes with some sort of light device, a stethoscope to the chest, a few taps with a rubber hammer, a couple of physical coordination exercises—and then said, "I see nothing to suggest that a referral to a neurologist is indicated. Your father isn't presenting anything unusual for a man his age."

Then why are you talking to me, *not him?* Caroline thought, but she didn't say it. She knew that the doctor was basing her judgment of

Mike on what she was seeing in front of her today. And Mike's vital signs and responses still fell within the "normal" range for a man his age. But Polcyk didn't know what was normal *for Mike*; she hadn't seen the changes that had been occurring. And, as Caroline tried to explain, it was the *changes* that were worrying her, as well as the speed of those changes. Caroline was kicking herself for not bringing her dad's notepads along as evidence.

"We tend to think of the aging process as steady and gradual," said Polcyk. "But sometimes changes occur in faster, more discrete clusters. And that's normal."

Caroline eye-signaled the doctor: *May I speak with you alone?* Polcyk picked up on the cue and stepped out of the room. "Aren't there any tests you can run," whispered Caroline to the doctor in the hall, "to see if he's developing Parkinson's or Alzheimer's or something else?"

"Unfortunately, no," replied Polcyk.

"What about a brain scan?"

"There's nothing to justify a costly procedure like that at this point."

"I've been doing some reading, and I know that early diagnosis can make all the difference." Since seeing her dad a month ago, Caroline had been conducting her own research into Parkinson's. She'd learned that Mike was showing several of the symptoms—a stooped walk, a quieter voice, changes in handwriting. She had also learned that the *progression* of the disease could be greatly slowed or arrested if treatment was done early. That was why someone like Michael J. Fox could stay at the same basic level for years, but other people deteriorated rapidly. Timing was critical.

"I'm sorry," said Dr. Polcyk. "I think your father is fine. But let's make a six-month appointment and look at him again."

"*Six months?* Can we make it sooner?"

"Six months should be sufficient."

Caroline was uncomfortable waiting that long, but she tried to take some reassurance from the fact that a doctor had examined him and said he was fine. That was good news, wasn't it?

Dr. Polcyk reentered the exam room and stood at the computer screen. She tried to project an air of confidence for the family, but she was feeling a trace of doubt. In truth, she was not *a neurologist, and the disorders the patient's daughter had mentioned were not her area of expertise—not by a medical-school mile—so she didn't know, with certainty, what tests might be currently available.*

What she did *know was that every time she ordered tests or referred a patient to a specialist, she had to fill out a form in "The System's" computer, and every quarter, she received a report showing the number of orders she had made compared to those made by her colleagues. No one had told her she was* required *to keep her referral numbers low, but she knew the unwritten rule. And she knew that in order to keep her job, she needed to play ball.*

With a silent sigh, she clicked the "next patient" button on the screen and told the Rennans, "I'll see you in six months." Even that, she knew, was probably not true. Mike Rennan would see whatever PCP happened to be on duty that day.

60

Over the next few months, Mike's condition deteriorated further. When Caroline would call home to speak to him, she found herself repeatedly asking him to speak louder. He developed a pronounced shuffle when he walked, and the tremor in his hand, which had previously bothered him only when he was writing, now became a constant companion. Even when his hand was dangling loosely at his side, it trembled. And it was starting to curl in a clawlike way.

Mike himself could no longer deny his concerns. One morning, a glance in the bedroom's full-length mirror made him gasp in shock. The stooped posture, the tremor, the bags under his eyes from lack of sleep, the masklike, almost angry expression that had crept over his face. Who *was* this guy?

Maybe it was time to let Marie and Caroline take him to a specialist.

After receiving a worried text message from her mom, Caroline called the medical group and was given another appointment with the PCP, just a few days away.

This time, when Dr. Polcyk examined Mike, she could not disguise her concern over Mike's tremors and his changed appearance and other symptoms.

I'd better send this man to a neurologist, *thought Dr. Polcyk. She realized she probably should have done so sooner, but failure to do so at this point could be considered malpractice (which meant she could lose not*

only her job but also her career). Not for the first or last time, she cursed the position she was in regarding referrals—damned if you do, damned if you don't.

And where did the patient's health stand in this whole formula?

With Dr. Polcyk's freshly written referral in hand, Caroline went downstairs to the front desk to schedule an appointment with a neurologist at the medical group.

"Would you like to see Dr. Adair, Dr. Howard, or Dr. Whalen?"

"Whoever can see him the soonest," replied Caroline.

She made her dad an appointment with Dr. Howard, the head of the neurology department. The appointment was still two weeks away, though, and both Caroline and her mom were worried about how much more Mike might deteriorate in that time.

Caroline kept thinking about Michael J. Fox and how his timely diagnosis had prevented him from developing more advanced symptoms.

61

Caroline drove her dad to the neurologist appointment. He had insisted that he could drive himself, but she was starting to become concerned about his driving. He often became forgetful about where he was going, not to mention his occasional loss of muscle control.

Mike and Caroline were taken to an exam room by an assistant, who asked a lot of questions and entered the data on a computer. When Dr. Howard, Triton's head of neurology, entered the room, she proceeded to ask many of the same questions the assistant had.

Because the computer screen was on the wall across from the exam table, the doctor barely looked at either Mike or Caroline as she asked her questions and logged their responses. *This room couldn't have been designed in a less patient-friendly way,* mused Caroline. *It's bizarre. Doesn't anyone notice this?*

Caroline made several attempts to point out her dad's latest symptoms to Dr. Howard: the new, stiff way he blinked his eyes, the nearly constant tremor in his right hand. But she found herself growing increasingly frustrated because the doctor didn't seem to be looking at her dad long enough to observe the symptoms herself.

All told, Dr. Howard spent about fifteen minutes with Mike, which was longer than the primary care doctor had, but not long enough, Caroline believed, for a thorough workup of her dad's condition—especially since the doctor spent most of that time looking at a computer rather than at Mike. The doctor didn't seem interested in anything Caroline had to say, either. As someone who had once planned to go to medical school herself, she believed she had valuable input to contribute. She had done a great deal of research into what she thought was wrong with her father.

"I know there are no definitive tests for Parkinson's," she said, "but aren't there some—"

Dr. Howard cut her off. "Tests won't be necessary. I can see what the issue is. Your father does have Parkinson's Disease, and it has started to advance."

Started to advance? Caroline was horrified and outraged. This was exactly what she had been afraid of. She knew there was medication that could substantially slow the disease, and the earlier it was started, the better. If her dad had been seen by a neurologist months ago when the family first contacted the clinic—instead of by a PCP, who had dead-ended Mike's treatment on the spot—his condition might not have advanced so quickly.

This was not OK! But it wasn't Dr. Howard's fault, she reminded herself, so it was pointless to be angry with her.

Dr. Howard wrote Mike a couple of prescriptions and said, "So we'll see you in six months for a recheck."

"Six months?" said Caroline in surprise, as she had to Dr. Polcyk. "Do you think that's wise? We've been seeing changes in him over just the past two or three months. Six months seems too long."

Howard nodded thoughtfully, as if weighing Caroline's concerns.

"Wouldn't two months—three months tops—be better?" she suggested.

Howard nodded again, turned back to the computer, and said goodbye.

Caroline and her dad took the prescriptions, thanked the doctor, and headed off to the scheduling area to make Mike's next appointment.

The scheduling desk was an elevator ride down to the first floor.

When the scheduler pulled up the doctor's notes, she said, "So Dr. Howard would like to see you again in six months."

"No," said Caroline. "That's a mistake. We talked about that. She agreed that two to three months made more sense."

"That's not what the doctor's notes say."

Caroline thought back to Dr. Howard's nod. Maybe it was more of an "I hear what you're saying" nod than an "I agree with you" nod.

"I can only go off the doctor's order as it appears in the computer," the scheduling person explained.

Caroline wanted to storm into Howard's office, but her office was a long distance away from the scheduling desk, both literally and figuratively.

"Six months is too long!" she said.

"I don't have the authority to change it," the scheduler explained. "If you want to be seen sooner, you'll have to talk to Dr. Howard again."

"May I?"

"You'll need to make another appointment."

"Another appointment! But we were just—"

"Never mind, sweetie," said Caroline's dad, taking her gently by the arm with his shaking hand. "Let's just take the appointment they're giving us."

Caroline agreed, just to spare her father further embarrassment.

62

When Caroline arrived home and investigated the medication the neurologist had prescribed, she learned it was *not* one of the newer and more effective medications on the market but instead a generic that had been around for years and had many known side effects. Concerned about this, she called the clinic and left a message for Dr. Howard.

It was three days before she heard back from her. During that time, Caroline didn't know if she should let her dad start taking the prescribed medicine or not, given the fact that he might be switching again, so she waited anxiously for the callback. When she finally spoke to Dr. Howard, she asked her point blank why she had not prescribed one of the two newer medications that had better reported results with fewer side effects.

"I was just trying to save your family money," she explained. "You see, those two medications you're talking about are not available as generics yet."

Did I ask you to save us money? thought Caroline, annoyed. She said, "Money isn't our main concern; my dad's health is. We'll pay for it out of pocket if need be."

Dr. Howard was silent for a moment. "I still think the meds I've prescribed are the best choice for him. They have a good track record over many years."

"But all of the literature says the new meds are better at slowing the progress of the disease."

"Literature isn't treating your father; *I* am. I've got a suggestion. I'm a trained neurologist with twenty years of experience. Why don't you let me determine which medications are best, and why don't you focus on giving your father the love and support he's going to need?"

Caroline could see that Dr. Howard wasn't going to budge. She did feel some relief, though, at hearing the doctor defend her choice of medications on treatment grounds, not just financial ones. Maybe (it was possible, right?) she knew what she was doing and Caroline should stop clicking around on medical websites.

Sometimes, Dr. Norma Howard must have felt as if she were under a microscope. Everything she did in her office—from the ordering of tests, procedures, and referrals to the writing of prescriptions—was tracked and monitored by the System.

Prescriptions were a particular focus of late. The System recorded how many prescriptions each doctor wrote, which meds they prescribed, and the total cost of their prescriptions. It also tracked the percentage of prescriptions that were for generics rather than brand names. Each quarter, each doctor received a report on their prescribing statistics compared to the other Triton doctors and to a "System Goal." In fact, her most recent report was sitting right on her desk.

> *Dear Physician,*
>
> *Enclosed is your Generic Prescribing Rate Report, which includes a comparison to others in your specialty and the medical group. Please remember, the "Generic Prescribing Program" is a* Pay for Performance *measure . . .*

"Pay for performance"—that meant that Coral Health received a financial incentive from the insurance companies when Triton doctors wrote generic prescriptions as opposed to name-brand orders. Like Dr.

Polcyk before her, Dr. Howard noted that none of the savings went into her pocket, but she knew that she needed to follow the rules if she wanted to keep her job.

Norma actually wanted to do more than stay employed. She was an ambitious woman who had designs on moving up in the medical group and even within the larger Coral Health system. She knew that the real money was made by the higher-ups—the medical directors, the management, the executives. And when doctors were promoted to those lofty positions, they not only made more money but also worked fewer hours, without the stress of seeing endless streams of patients.

Norma Howard was on her way toward her goal. She had been appointed director of the neurology department just a year before and was slated for the board of directors soon. She couldn't afford to mess this opportunity up. And if writing generic prescriptions was her ticket out of the grind of daily patient care, she was going to write away.

63

Caroline and her mom accompanied Mike to the six-month follow-up appointment Dr. Howard had scheduled. Mike could no longer drive at all, owing to his symptoms and to the side effects of the medication he'd been taking for half a year now. One of these side effects, for Mike, was narcolepsy; he could drop off to sleep anytime, anywhere, regardless of what he was doing.

Today's exam was almost an exact replay of the previous one. Dr. Howard stared at the computer screen most of the time, glancing at Mike only occasionally. Caroline pointed out that Mike had begun habitually rubbing his thumb and forefinger together.

"That's called the 'pill-rolling tremor,'" said Howard in a neutral tone. She didn't say whether this was cause for concern or not.

Caroline pointed out that her dad's bouts of dizziness had gotten worse, too. Howard did not respond.

The doctor did finally say, "I'd like to examine your gait and balance, Mr. Rennan, so please put on an exam gown. I'll be back in a moment."

Dr. Howard left the room, and Caroline and Mrs. Rennan exited behind her. Caroline thought the doctor was leaving just long enough to give her dad some privacy, but then she heard Howard's voice from another exam room, saying, "I'm Dr. Howard. What brings you in today?"

She was seeing other patients.

It was fifteen minutes before the neurologist returned to the Rennans' room. At that point, she asked Mike to walk across the room and to stand with his arms out. She shot Mike a few questions: "Do you feel dizzy?" and "Does one leg feel weaker than the other?" The "exam" was over within thirty seconds. At its conclusion, Howard went back to the computer and did some more clicking and typing. The printer then spat up a refill of Mike's prescriptions, which Dr. Howard handed to Mike.

"Oh, I was hoping we could talk about his meds first," said Caroline. "He's been falling asleep constantly in the middle of the day, and I know that's a side effect."

"It could be age-related, too," said Dr. Howard. "It's fairly common in older people."

"But it's only been happening since he started on this medication," said Caroline.

"Your father is in his mid-sixties," replied Dr. Howard in a mildly exasperated tone, "and he has a progressive illness." Howard then stood up abruptly, saying, "See you next time," with a tight smile, and exited the room, leaving Mike with a refill of the old medication and Caroline with her blood simmering.

Norma Howard had to feel a sting of guilt as she hurried to her next exam room. She probably should have talked to the family more about Mr. Rennan's medications, but she had already closed the chart. "Closing the chart"—that was another way Triton and Coral Health were monitoring doctors for speed and efficiency. It was bad enough that doctors had to triple-book patients and send them out the door in record time—"through-put" was God at Triton—but now the MDs were also given a limited time window in which to complete all the entries in the patients' EMRs. Entries also had to be coded a certain way for billing purposes, which meant documenting multiple ailments and checking boxes all over the multisection

chart—*all of which, of course, took time and attention. And if doctors didn't "close the chart" within the time required, that was grounds for discipline.*

As irritated as this might have made Dr. Howard, she was doubly committed to doing everything by the book in the hopes of moving up the ladder ASAP and into the rarefied ranks of the doctors who sat on the management team. She couldn't wait.

When the Rennans went downstairs to make their next appointment, they learned that, once again, it wasn't scheduled till another six months out.

"This is ridiculous!" shouted Caroline to the woman at the desk.

"Shh, honey, that's just the way it is," said Mrs. Rennan, ushering her daughter toward the door with an embarrassed look over her shoulder.

Fine. Caroline would leave peacefully, but she loved her dad too much to see him continuing to deteriorate without getting the help she knew was out there.

She was going to do something about this.

64

Two cups of Tension Tamer tea were not enough to calm Caroline down. She was still incensed about Dr. Howard's attitude, which she perceived as arrogance. She was going to find a new neurologist, period. One who would actually care—or would at least do a better job of pretending.

She set out to investigate what her options were. She learned there were three other neurologists within her dad's medical group. The youngest of them, Dr. Whalen, was close to Caroline's own age. She wondered if a younger doctor might be more open to trying the latest modes of treatment. She also noted that Dr. Walen specialized in Parkinson disease. She wondered if he might give her dad better care.

Decision made.

She contacted the medical group and asked to transfer her dad's care to Dr. Whalen. She was expecting some pushback from Triton—they always pushed back, it seemed—but they were agreeable this time, probably because it was a lateral move.

Dr. Bob Whalen took over Mike Rennan's care. The Rennans immediately loved him. He spent *time* with Mike. He asked a lot of questions and actually *listened to his answers*, and those of the family, rather than focusing on the computer screen.

The family even saw some improvement in Mike's condition. Probably because Dr. Whalen switched him to one of the newer meds, one that had fewer side effects and was more effective in slowing the disease's progression. Mike definitely seemed less dizzy, which meant he was much less likely to have a fall. And that made both Mike and his family feel a lot more confident about his continued independence.

Dr. Whalen saw Mike Rennan six times over course of the next year and half—every three months, not every six. Not only did he see him more *often*, but he also saw him for longer visits. As opposed to the fifteen minutes or fewer that Dr. Howard had allotted, Dr. Whalen spent at least forty-five minutes with Mike each time.

The new doctor also initiated a practice of asking Mike and the family to complete a questionnaire each time they arrived at the clinic. The questionnaire asked for details about how Mike was doing, on a one to ten scale, with a host of physical activities, symptoms, and side effects. This allowed Dr. Whalen to efficiently gather detailed information from the family so that he could spend more of the actual visit giving visual attention to Mike and observing how he was doing.

Caroline knew Parkinson's disease didn't have a cure, but at least she now felt that her dad was getting the best care possible.

This impression was strengthened by the way Dr. Whalen went to bat for his patients. When he first took over Mike's care, he ordered an MRI so he could see exactly how far his disease had progressed. The service was denied, so Dr. Whalen appealed the decision, first to Coral Health and then to the insurance company itself. Eventually, the MRI was authorized.

Later, Dr. Whalen tried to have Mike approved for physical therapy to help him with his balance. Again, payment for the service was denied. But Caroline received a call one evening from Dr. Whalen himself—not from an office staffer—saying that Whalen was personally fighting to appeal that denial.

In this day and age of shrinking personal care, Caroline felt she couldn't do any better than to have Dr. Whalen on her family's team.

65

Bob Whalen eyed the e-mail again. *Management wanted to have a meeting with him. Crap. Well, he couldn't say he hadn't seen it coming. The parade of memos had been picking up momentum of late, and Bob knew he was drawing the ire of a few members of the management team.*

Why? It wasn't as if he was doing a poor job as a doctor. Quite the contrary. He believed, in his mind and in his heart, that he was doing excellent work with his patients. He was a thorough, caring, and conscientious physician, and he knew it.

But somewhere along the line, his job description had shifted subtly. It was no longer about putting patient care first; it was about increasing productivity—whatever that meant in a medical setting—and reducing costs.

Actually, Bob knew exactly *when the change had happened. A few years ago, the clinic had been purchased by Coral Health. Prior to that time, he had been one of the staff's shining stars, thanks to his high-level skills with diagnosis and treatment. But since then, his star had been fading.*

A new executive team had been hired, and the new focus was on efficiency. The model the management team had adopted was called "Lean." It was all about eliminating waste and moving patients through treatment as quickly, cheaply, and cleanly as possible—almost like an assembly line. That meant cutting back on everything: time, attention, expense. The bosses could not come right out and ask doctors to reduce patient care, but that was what they pushed for at every staff meeting and in every policy they issued. Bob did not believe this new system was good for patients, and he was not shy about expressing his opinion.

214

There were several areas where Bob and his new employers were at odds. One of these revolved around the handling of EMRs. Bob liked to spend as much face time as possible with his patients, not with a computer. For that reason, he preferred to use his appointments to talk to patients and observe them. He would update the EMRs after the exam—which usually meant doing so on evenings and Saturdays, because he typically fell behind during his workday.

Bob would have thought management would be delighted by the fact that he did his record keeping on his own time, but no. They had determined, as part of the Lean system, that all records needed to be completed and closed while the patient was present. It didn't make sense, but neither did many of Coral Health's new policies.

The reason Bob fell behind in his workday was because of another new policy, one that called for the shortening of patient visits. Even though he repeatedly told the schedulers that he wanted his appointments—especially for new patients—to be scheduled for sixty-minute slots, he constantly found that they gave him thirty minutes instead. That wasn't enough time to do the necessary observation and evaluation, so Dr. Whalen's appointments would routinely run over. As a result, he would quickly fall behind. He complained about the schedulers not complying with his instructions, but he was told by his bosses that he was "making unreasonable demands on staff."

Length *of patients' appointments was not the only issue; frequency was another area where Dr. Whalen was often at loggerheads with his bosses. Bob was told to see patients every six months, and he didn't feel that was often enough. With some neurological conditions, patients might need to be seen every two to four* weeks, *others every three months. But six months was too long, in any case; a disease like Parkinson's progresses too fast. You're always behind it, trying to catch up.*

Medications were yet another issue. Coral Health's Generic Prescribing Program had very strict "suggestions" about which medications the doctors should be prescribing. These were, of course, the older and cheaper generics. Bob knew that the newer meds were often better and had fewer side effects, but they didn't have generic counterparts yet. So they cost more money—for the insurance company. The insurer didn't like that, and neither did Coral Health. Even when generics were available, Bob didn't always want to use the officially "preferred" ones. Some patients tolerated one generic better than another. The bottom line was that Bob wanted the freedom to prescribe what was best for his patients, whether that meant using a name-brand medication or choosing one generic over another. And so he often exercised that freedom, to his bosses' chagrin.

Bob and his bosses even disagreed about reminder calls to patients. Bob liked to have his nursing staff personally call family members with reminders about upcoming appointments. The bosses didn't like this. "It takes too much staff time; that's why we have robocalls," they said. But, as Bob would point out to them, robocalls don't work well for patients with dementia or memory issues. Robocalls go directly to the patient, and patients often miss them, ignore them, or forget them. Bob preferred to talk to the actual family member responsible for driving the patient to the appointment. But the bosses said no, insisting on robocalls only. As a result, many patients missed their appointments. And anytime a patient missed an appointment, it meant they weren't getting the care they needed. A missed appointment could even be fatal.

Lastly, Bob refused to follow the System's "guidelines" (read: rules) regarding referrals. He ordered tests, treatments, and referrals to others physicians—inside or outside the System—as he saw fit, based on his standards of good medical care. And when the medical directors denied these services as "not medically necessary," he appealed the denials. He was a bona fide pain in the rear about this. He knew the bosses were keeping track of such "leakage," but patient care was primary to Bob, and he assumed all of the doctors in the system felt the same way.

Wrong assumption, as it turned out.

66

The day of the disciplinary meeting arrived. Bob assumed it was just going to be the informal toe-the-line lecture he'd been expecting for a while. He didn't think it would be any more serious than that, because he knew he had extremely high patient satisfaction ratings. But when he walked into the conference room, he saw Triton's chief medical director and three men and women in suits he didn't recognize arranged around the table, looking grim. In front of each attendee was a printout of a chart showing Bob's referrals, test orders, and prescription costs as compared to the other doctors.

Bob was shown the chart, and it became starkly apparent to him that not all of the other doctors in the System actually did put patient care first; most of them, it seemed, played ball with Coral Health. Maybe Bob really was an outlier here.

"You're being placed on a PIP," said one of the suits.

"OK . . . and what's a PIP?"

"Performance Improvement Plan," another suit said.

"Performance improvement? What on Earth for?" asked Bob, stunned. This kind of disciplinary action was not only personally humiliating but would also look terrible on his record. "How am I not performing? I haven't had one patient complaint."

The doctors and executives exchanged uncomfortable looks.

"What is this really about?" asked Bob.

"Patient care is primary at Triton, of course," said the medical director. Sure, thought Bob. "But there are other considerations. The fact is, we can't run a profitable business unless we keep expenditures within certain parameters. *We have been explaining this* at length *at staff and physician meetings. At length.*"

"*Are you saying I should go against my better medical judgment and withhold services that I believe my patients need?*"

"*No one is saying that,*" *replied the medical director.* Of course not, *thought Bob,* because you know you'd be in legal trouble if you said that. "*And we're not questioning your judgment in any specific case.*"

"*Then what exactly* are *you saying?*" *He wanted to pin them down on this.*

"*Come on, Bob,*" *said one of the suits.* "*Don't be obtuse. What we need is for you to become more of a team player.*"

"*I want to be told specifically why I'm being put on a PIP when my* performance as a doctor—*which, last I checked, was my job here—has been excellent.*"

"*You'll be receiving some follow-up materials,*" *said the medical director, tersely.* "*I sincerely hope you give them careful thought.*" *The executive team rose and filed out of the room.*

Over the next few months, Bob did indeed receive materials. A week didn't pass that there wasn't something new in his inbox. He received "utilization reviews," graphs, and pie charts that continued to show that he was ordering more tests, more referrals, and more expensive medications than his peers. He received copies of clinic policies regarding the approved length (thirty minutes) and frequency (six months) of patient visits. He received reminders about the Generic Prescribing Program. And, of course, he received memos telling him he was still out of step with the "team."

Through it all, Bob refused to compromise. He wasn't deliberately trying to anger his bosses, but he continued to use good patient care as his guiding principle.

The frequency and heat of the memos continued to increase, and one day, after receiving a particularly nasty memo, Bob had had enough. He finally realized that, despite his excellent medical reputation, he simply wasn't valued at Triton. He didn't like being a perennial troublemaker, and he didn't like being in constant friction with his peers. He picked up the phone and called his boss.

"Dr. Howard, this just isn't working out for either of us. I think I'm a good doctor; evidently you disagree. So what I'd like to do is request a transfer to the east-side clinic." Bob was thinking that maybe the problem was just one of personalities involved. He might get along better at a new site.

"I'll take that into consideration and get back to you."

A week or two later, Bob received an e-mail telling him that a meeting had been set up to address his concerns. Good. He went through his day feeling lighthearted for the first time in months.

When the meeting rolled around, Bob was surprised to find the same grim "tribunal" in the room as at the last meeting.

"The MEC"—medical executive committee—"has conducted a review of your care of five patients," announced the medical director.

What? This was news to Bob. No one had informed him that such an investigation had been undertaken. He was shocked.

But he was positively floored by what he heard next.

"As a result of the review," the medical director continued, "a recommendation was made to terminate you. So, basically, you have three options. You can either resign, which will require you to sign a confidentiality agreement; accept a termination 'without cause'; or you can fight us, in which case you'll be terminated 'with cause.'"

"And that means that the MEC will issue a formal report on its

findings," chimed in one of the suits, "which will be reportable to the state medical board."

Bob thought his jaw was going to hit the table. A report to the medical board could lead to him losing his medical license. Even termination "without cause" could haunt him for life and destroy his career—he'd heard about the "blackball" effect some of his peers had experienced.

Bob asked to be excused and dashed out into the hallway. Leaning on the wall, he took several deep breaths to relieve his dizziness. Once he recovered from the initial shock, it didn't take him five minutes to realize that he really had no choice about which course of action to take. He resigned his position and was out the door in thirty days.

67

Caroline brought her dad in for his scheduled exam with Dr. Whalen. When they checked in at the front desk, the receptionist said, "Your father will be seen by Dr. Adair today."

"Who is that?" asked Caroline.

"He's one of our other neurologists."

Caroline didn't want her dad to see a strange doctor, but she also didn't want him to fall behind in his treatment. Knowing that rescheduling would mean a delay of weeks, if not months, the Rennans reluctantly accepted the appointment.

The exam was quick and cursory, like Dr. Howard's had been. As it was going on, Caroline asked the doctor whether Dr. Whalen was OK, thinking that maybe he was just out sick for the day.

"Yes, he's fine," replied Dr. Adair, not elaborating further.

It wasn't until the Rennans went downstairs to make their next appointment that the scheduling person told her, "Oh, Dr. Whalen is no longer here."

"What do you mean? Where did he go? Do you have a new address or phone number for him?"

"I can't give out that information."

"I thought you were *required* to give it out, actually. So that patients can have the option of continuing with the same doctor if they choose."

The scheduler looked flustered and said, "You can talk to someone in administration, if you'd like."

Caroline went upstairs but had no better luck there. When the office receptionist echoed what the scheduler had told her, Caroline said, "I'd like to speak to someone in charge."

A woman in a suit barreled out of an office in the back corner and repeated the party line, "We can't give you that information."

"Dr. Whalen borrowed some medical books to us and I need to return them," said Caroline. This wasn't true, but Caroline hoped the ploy would pry the information free.

"Give them to me, and I'll make sure he gets them."

Caroline went home and Googled Dr. Whalen. According to the website, he was still working at Triton Medical Group. *Why don't they ever update these listings?* she wondered. She felt a surge of anger at the medical group for assigning a new neurologist without even discussing it with her. She also felt anger toward Dr. Whalen, along with disappointment. Perhaps Caroline had been wrong to hold Whalen in such high regard. *If he were really such a great doctor, he wouldn't have abandoned his patient.*

About six months after Bob left Triton, his former employer finally posted a link to his new website, and some of his former patients started to find him. They all told him the same story—that when they'd called Triton to make an appointment, they were not told Dr. Whalen had left; they were simply told they needed to select a new doctor. Since Dr. Whalen was still listed on Coral Health's website, they assumed he had taken time off or was practicing at another location within the system. Bob suspected this was more than a mere oversight. He thought Coral Health was deliberately making

it hard for his patients to find him, while continuing to pad the ranks of their approved neurologists. Ah well, good riddance to them. Triton and Coral Health were part of his past.

Establishing his own practice had been tougher than he'd thought, though. He had tried to contract with health insurance companies, but when he saw the rates of reimbursement they were offering him—which were very low because he did not have the negotiating power of a large group—he was appalled. After crunching the numbers with his accountant, he realized he wouldn't be able to make it financially if he "took insurance." The only way he could continue to practice medicine was either to go to work as an employee again—and, frankly, he'd rather have gouged his eyes out—or convert his business model to a new and upcoming model: a concierge practice.

So he did the latter. Almost two years after leaving Triton, Bob was happy in his new practice. He loved his patients and had "moved on." When he thought about Triton, he was still furious about how they'd treated him, but he never gave serious consideration to suing them or Coral Health.

Until the day he got the phone call.

68

"Bob? This is Kaitlin. Kaitlin Smith."

"Oh, hi." Kaitlin was a nurse Bob had worked with years earlier, and they still kept in touch. Why was Kaitlin calling him on a Sunday?

"You used to treat Mike Rennan, right?" Kaitlin asked.

"Yes, nice man. And a very sweet family," Bob replied. Then Bob recalled that Kaitlin knew the Rennans personally. "But of course, you know that."

"I'm wondering if I can ask you a favor on behalf of the family. A pretty big favor, actually."

"What is it?"

"Mike collapsed at a family picnic today."

"Oh my God, I'm so sorry to hear that."

"He's at Valley Medical and he's not doing well at all."

"Mike's not a patient of mine anymore," said Bob. "I think he's with Ken Adair now. And besides, I don't have treating privileges at Valley Medical." That hospital was part of the Coral Health system Bob had left the previous year.

"I know that, but . . . they're ready to pull the plug on Mike, and the family would really appreciate it."

"Pull the plug? Good God. Give me twenty minutes."

Kaitlin met Bob in the lobby and caught him up on the particulars of the case as they briskly walked to Mike Rennan's room.

"They called 911 right away, and someone did CPR until the paramedics got there."

"How soon did they arrive?" asked Bob.

"Pretty quickly, I'm told. The good news is, we don't have to guess about the time. One of his grandchildren took a video of the whole thing on his phone."

"Excellent. Have you looked at Mike?"

"Yeah. Not good. Adair was in a while ago, and he's telling the family Mike's brain dead and there's nothing that can be done."

"Good lord, it seems a little premature for that, don't you think?"

"That's why I called you."

When Bob arrived at the Rennans' room, Caroline and Marie Rennan were standing over Mike's bed, looking ashen. The ER doctor was there, too, so Bob addressed him. "Can I have a look at the MRI?"

"Um, there isn't one," said the doctor, looking a bit embarrassed.

"What?" said Bob, incredulous. "Why not?"

"I ran it by Dr. Adair, and he said he wasn't able to order one."

"Because?"

"Authorization was denied by the system," said the ER physician. "I'm sorry, but without authorization, there's nothing I can do."

"Well, there's something I can do," Bob said, flashing more anger than he intended. He turned to the family and said, "If you'll have your dad transferred to Mercy Hospital, where I have treating privileges, I will order an MRI right away and take over his treatment."

The family agreed, and Bob immediately made arrangements for Mike's transfer. While he waited for the ambulance, he asked to see the grandchild's picnic video on the smartphone. The time between Mike's collapse and the arrival of the EMTs had been less than five minutes. There was every reason to think that Mike still had a fighting chance. The denial of the MRI—just to save money for Coral Health—was an unconscionable decision that might easily have cost this man his life.

When Bob arrived at home, he was still enraged. Triton had put one of his former patients' lives at risk. Bob could not, in good conscience, stand by and watch this happen. It was one thing to mess with Bob's career; it was another thing to mess with people's lives.

He picked up the phone and called a lawyer friend of his. "Jerry, do you know any good employment lawyers?"

Bob had decided to sue.

PART VIII

A Neurologist's Tale

The Lawsuit

69

As a rule, I never take a case without meeting the client. Often, we'll have several phone conversations and e-mail exchanges as I explore the case, but I never give the final thumbs-up or thumbs-down without an in-person meeting.

In this case, I received a call from Doug, a trusted doctor client of mine, who was referring the client to me.

"I gotta warn you," Doug said after filling me in on the basics, "you'll be going up against Coral Health. They're the Teflon Giant; nothing sticks to these guys."

Coral Health was a large and influential "health-care system," not an insurance company or medical group. These health "systems" were relatively new players in the health-care delivery scene, and many of them were corporate goliaths. I knew that suing one of them would have its unique challenges.

"Bob's a good doctor," Doug told me. "An excellent doctor. He's not a troublemaker or an axe grinder; this really is a matter of conscience for him."

When I spoke to Bob himself, I learned that his story was one I'd heard many times before.

"I was just trying to do my job," he said. "And my job, as a physician, is to give my patients the best care possible, or at least present all the options to them. But Coral Health was putting all these policies in place that didn't allow me to do my job. And so, when I started putting good patient care ahead of corporate policies, the bosses turned *me* into the bad guy and forced me out. I couldn't believe it—I had the highest patient satisfaction ratings."

Ah, yes. The details may vary, but the basic storyline is always the same.

"So why you do want to sue, Bob? What's your true motive here?"

"It's not about me," he said. "It's really not. I've moved on. My new practice is doing very well, and I don't have time for negative energy in my life, but I feel I *have* to do something or I won't be able to live with myself. I know patients who are being put at risk *as we speak*, and I know other doctors at Triton who are getting the squeeze exactly like I did. It's not OK to treat people this way."

He shared with me several stories of patients being medically harmed and doctors being forced out of the group, either by conscience, by threat, or by actually being fired.

After we spoke, he sent me a FedEx packet—a pretty thin one—containing copies of his employment contract and a few e-mails he'd saved. They weren't much, but they seemed to back up the truth of his story.

There was a sense of urgency in filing this particular lawsuit, because Dr. Whalen had waited almost two years after his termination before contacting me, and this type of suit has a two-year statute of limitations. In a sense, it was the lateness of the filing that tipped the scales for me. His motive was obviously not financial self-interest or payback. If either of those had been his reasons, he would have filed sooner. His motivation really was bigger than himself; it was about stopping wrongful practices that he had observed to be hurting people. *If he's willing to put himself on the line to stop these practices,* I thought to myself, *I want to throw my skills and experience behind him.*

I picked up the phone and called him. "Bob, I'm going to do something I've never done before. I'm going to accept your case without a face-to-face meeting. I think we need to get moving on this thing. Now."

70

A few problems emerged when I started to write the "complaint"—that's the document that initiates the lawsuit. I'm pretty nitpicky when it comes to writing complaints. I like them to tell the most detailed and accurate story possible. That's because I know the defendants will immediately file an aggressive motion—called a *demurrer*—to dismiss my claims, so I factor in their response from the start. I want my complaint to robustly withstand the first round of slings and arrows.

Details were going to be a challenge in this case, though. When Dr. Whalen had "resigned" from the medical group, his bosses had not allowed him to take *anything* with him—not so much as a sticky note. All I had for documentation was a copy of his employment contract and a few e-mails that he had thought to forward to himself after his fateful meeting. I had virtually no paper from Coral Health, the defendant. That was a problem, because I usually rely on such documents to put the bones of the story together—dates, names of relevant individuals, chronologies, that type of thing. Often, the doctors themselves—my clients—don't recall all the specifics, because 1) they were not planning on filing a lawsuit when the events happened, and 2) they were focused on taking care of their patients. That was certainly true of Dr. Whalen. But as an added challenge in Bob's case, more than two years had passed since most of the events had occurred, so his recollection was even foggier than most doctors'.

That wasn't my biggest problem, though. The biggest problem was that the defendant had structured itself into three separate legal entities. I knew that in reality it was all "one big family," as its website proudly proclaimed, but the legal structure was a hurdle. It had been set up in such a way to dodge the very type of lawsuit I was planning to bring. And I didn't want the main culprit—Coral Health, the parent company—to weasel out of this on a technicality.

The technicality was that only one of the three entities, Triton Medical Group, was Bob's *actual* employer. Getting around this road-block was going to be tricky.

A little background here. In the "old days," doctors owned their own practices. They owned the buildings, employed the staff, accepted payments from patients, and paid their bills. Then, as health insurance began to dominate the health-care landscape more and more, doctors began to form medical groups. The advantage to this arrangement was that large groups of doctors had more bargaining power with insurance companies when negotiating fees. These medical groups grew larger and larger. With the kind of money that was eventually involved, it was only natural that corporate America would want to stick its fingers into that pie.

The problem for the corporate folks is that there are laws in many states that prohibit the "corporate practice of medicine." In other words, legally, it's not permissible for medical groups to be owned by non-doctors. The idea is that doctors shouldn't be pressured by businesspeople when making medical decisions. The corporate practice of medicine, it is believed, would undermine the physician–patient relationship and interfere with the independent medical judgment of the physician.

Since a corporation can't own a medical group, they get around the law by forming these health systems. The *system* becomes the entity that negotiates with the insurance company for dollars. The system then turns around and contracts with a medical group to provide the medical services. I believe it's the "corporate practice of medicine," just set up in a way that's technically legal.

In Bob's particular case, the structure was a three-part one. The system, Coral Health, created an affiliate company, Coral Health Partners, to provide all of the support services for its clinics—i.e., employing the nurses and receptionists, doing the schedules and payroll, and owning the buildings and medical equipment. The *affiliate* then contracted separately with Triton Medical Group for just the "physicians' services" component. Triton was technically owned by doctors. Technically.

The way patient care becomes compromised in this kind of business arrangement is that all of the money comes in to the top (i.e., into the "system") rather than to the doctors themselves. These big "systems" receive huge contracts from insurers to provide *all* the healthcare services for huge pools of patients for a fixed dollar amount. We're talking contracts worth millions and millions of dollars. The system (e.g., Coral Health), being financially motivated, wants to retain as much of that money as it can. In simple terms, that means that the amount of money the system spends on patient care has to be less than the amount it takes in from the insurer. This is why we see all these new policies trying to limit spending on medical tests, referrals, prescriptions, and other patient services. It is also why the system creates incentives for the medical groups it contracts with, telling them, in effect, "Save us money on services, and we'll give you a bonus; *cost* us money on services, and you'll owe us money."

This is not a model for providing great medical care. The underlying business motive is always to give the patients less so that the system can keep more.

And, as a result of the ownership and management setup, it appears to me that the system is the real boss. The system tells the medical group what to do, and the medical group tells the doctors what to do. In every meaningful way, the system employs the doctors. But officially, the doctors work for the medical group. In reality, "non-doctors" *are* running the show, and they *are* undermining the physicians' exercise of independent medical judgment.

So my problem was: How could I sue Coral Health, the parent health system, and its affiliate, Coral Health Partners, when they were not technically Dr. Whalen's employer? As I researched this issue, I discovered that many doctors over the years had tried to sue Coral Health, but the company had always skated away on the legal technicality that it was "not the doctors' employer."

I needed to find a new and different legal theory than everyone had used in the past. Piece of cake. Ha.

I laced up my running shoes and hit the pavement. I do my best thinking when I'm running around Balboa Island, near my home.

71

Try as I might, I couldn't come up with an angle that would work. So much for the magic of running.

I was getting near the end of my run when I passed a pedestrian wearing a T-shirt advertising one of the new medical marijuana dispensaries that were popping up all over California. Its name was The Joint Venture.

I stopped dead in my tracks. A light bulb had ignited in my mind for some reason, but I couldn't put my finger on why. I started moving again and ran home in double time.

By the time I made it back to my home office, my vague intuition had gelled into a real idea. Maybe I could build my strategy for suing around a concept called "joint venture liability." I had used it years earlier in a non-doctor's case. The heart of the theory is this: if two or more entities are involved in a joint venture, when one of the parties does something wrong, all of the parties are equally liable.

What is this joint venture? Well, if I were to explain it to a jury, I might use the example of three guys robbing a bank (since three is the number of entities we're dealing with here). One guy is the hold-up person, a second guy is the getaway car driver, and a third is the lookout. They all do different jobs, but they're all working together toward a certain end. If the venture succeeds, they're all going to enjoy some of the money. Maybe the hold-up guy takes 50 percent, and the other two take 25 percent each. And maybe the hold-up guy is the most blameworthy. But if they are arrested, they're all equally culpable, and they all go to jail for the same amount of time. They are all equally punished.

The same applies when suing three parties for joint venture liability. If wrong is done and damages occur, it doesn't matter if one of the parties is 90 percent responsible and the other two parties are only 5 percent each; all three are considered "jointly and severally liable"—any one of them (or all of them) can be sued for the full amount.

I believed this principle might be the key to holding Coral Health accountable for its actions. In order to claim joint venture liability in this case, I first needed to prove that a joint venture actually existed amongst the three entities—the System (Coral Health), the Affiliate (Coral Health Partners), and the Medical Group (Triton). To be considered a joint venture, three criteria must be met: 1) There is an agreement in place that the parties are working together toward a certain end. That agreement doesn't necessarily have to be in writing. It can be verbal, or it can simply be implied by the parties' behaviors. 2) There is some measure of joint control. That is, all three parties have some say in how business is conducted—though that control need not be evenly distributed. 3) There is a sharing of profits and/or losses—again, not necessarily evenly divided.

So I decided to sue all three parties with this concept in mind.

Coral Health and Coral Health Partners hired the same legal team and basically functioned as a single defendant. Triton, the medical group, hired a different legal team.

Of course, the first thing the Coral Health team did was file a demurrer saying, in effect, "You can't sue us. You're going after the wrong parties because: 1) we didn't employ the doctor, and 2) we didn't have anything to do with this doctor."

My response to the demurrer was essentially, *That's exactly why I am using the joint venture theory!*

The medical group, Triton, took a different position from Coral's. It said, "The doctor was not terminated, he resigned." That was technically true. The law, however, allows for something called "constructive wrongful termination," which means that sometimes a person, while technically resigning, is actually forced to resign. It's a difficult legal position to take, though, with a high bar of proof required.

I was going out on a limb with my joint venture theory, and I knew it. I had no idea how the judge would react to it. To my pleasant surprise, he rejected the defendants' demurrers and agreed that our complaint had sufficient merit to go to trial.

We were a go. The lawsuit was on.

72

Now it was time for discovery. The usual dance took place: I requested material; they failed to give it to me. This happens every time, like clockwork.

Coral Health's lawyers refused to respond to any of my discovery requests, because they continued to maintain that Coral Health had "nothing to do with the doctor" and that I was propounding discovery on the "wrong parties." They took the position that Triton was a completely separate entity from Coral Health. So they refused to produce any documents or answer any of my interrogatories or cooperate in any way. They stonewalled me, acting as if I didn't exist.

It was not until a year into the lawsuit and after many, many motions to the court that I finally was able to obtain some *very limited* documents from Coral Health. And even then, they produced only documents I'd already found on the Internet; they essentially gave me nothing. Their lawyers didn't even bother to show up to the depositions I took of Triton doctors or to my client's deposition.

Triton's lawyers took the opposite tack. They inundated me with paper. They gave me over twenty thousand pages of documents, and for every thousand pages they gave me, there were really only eighty pages of actual material; the rest were duplicates of long e-mail strings or duplicates of duplicates of duplicates. But despite the "document dump" approach by its lawyers, it almost seemed as if *Triton itself* was secretly trying to help me. Because when I did find needles buried in the haystack, they turned out to be invaluable.

One example was a PowerPoint presentation called "Leakage." From what I could gather, this document had been created by someone within Coral Health and had been shown to the doctors at Triton. It was remarkable both for its bad taste and its starkly money-driven agenda. The document was all about creating "greater retention of income" for Coral Health while reducing "expenses" (i.e., paying for patient treatments). The cover of the document was, astonishingly, a full-page photo of a public bathroom with eighteen inches of raw sewage flooding the floor and one word: "Leakage." Wow.

It was so crass, on more than one level, that it almost couldn't be real. When I showed it to my husband, he said, "I wouldn't touch that. They're just trying to set you up. No one would really have created or shown a PowerPoint like that."

That was my sense, too. Surely this thing was a "plant" to make me look bad; if I were to use it in court, I would be ridiculed for even thinking it was real. But . . . if it *was* real, I thought it would play very powerfully with a jury. It essentially equated the money spent on patient care with spilled excrement. If a picture is worth a thousand words, this one was worth a million. A billion.

I needed to track down the source of the document. You see, the mere fact that I find a document in a pile of material the defendant turns over to me doesn't necessarily mean I can use it in court. I still have to prove its authenticity. That means I have to be able to first establish *what the document is*—in this case, that it was a PowerPoint that was actually shown within the organization. Then I have to prove that it is an accurate and truthful version of that document, one that hadn't been altered. I also need to show "foundation," which means I need to find someone who is in a position to testify as to the nature and accuracy of the document. In most cases, that would be the author of the piece.

When I asked Coral Health about the document, the defendants were predictably unhelpful. "We have thousands of employees; we have no way of tracking down who made some PowerPoint document years ago."

I did manage to find out that the PowerPoint doc had been shown at a shareholders' meeting, but I couldn't convince anyone to admit to having seen it. As I deposed witness after witness, I would show them this monstrosity and ask, "Have you ever seen this?" They would laugh and say no.

Coral Health's lawyers began to roll their eyes every time I trotted it out. "You're not going to find anyone who saw that; it's obviously phony."

But I had come to believe it was *not* phony, and I was determined to track down its source. Finally, when one manager was testifying at her deposition, she looked at the PowerPoint and said, "Oh, *I* remember that thing. I'll tell you why. Our shareholders' meetings are held in the evening over dinner. We had just been served our meals when someone put that slide up on the projector, and I remember thinking, Who on Earth wants to look at *that* while they're eating?"

I'd finally found someone who could at least testify that the PowerPoint was real and had been shown within the company. From there, I was able to track down the author. The funny thing was, he didn't see anything wrong with the document. He seemed even a little bit proud of it.

But I had the feeling that once a jury saw a glimpse of this thing—and the corporate mind-set behind it—I would be halfway to winning this case.

73

Many other documents produced by Triton—buried in their document dump—also helped me figure out how heavily involved Coral Health was in the actual management of Triton doctors. These documents clearly revealed to me that it was Coral Health that had originated the policies, taken the actions to implement them, enforced them, and punished the doctors who did not follow them.

The interesting thing was that only *Triton* was giving me these documents. They should have been produced by Coral Health. The documents, after all, were on Coral Health letterhead and were signed and authored by Coral Health people. But whenever I'd send document requests to Coral Health, their people would claim, under sworn statement, "We don't have those documents." Right. Why would the doctors' group have all this stuff while Coral Health, the authors, did not?

The fact that Triton kept supplying these documents to me while Coral Health refused suggested that maybe the Triton folks really didn't like Coral Health very much. Maybe they didn't appreciate this new parent company interfering with their medical practice any more than my client, Bob Whalen, did. Maybe that's why they seemed to be subtly, perhaps unconsciously, feeding me ammunition.

Coral Health undoubtedly thought it was hampering my case by stonewalling me. But the truth of the matter is that I was more than happy to watch a defendant stonewall. You see, experience had taught me that eventually, if I kept digging, I would find out that Coral Health *did*, in fact, have copies of all these documents. They had to; they created them. And when the time came for me to ask them, in court, why they hadn't given these docs to me, they would have to come up with some kind of justification, such as, "Oh, those were confidential and we couldn't share them."

To which I would respond, "But that's not what you said in your sworn statement, signed by your Executive VP. You said that you *didn't have them.*" And there'd be no way for them to wiggle out of their own sworn statement.

And when a party in court fails to produce evidence that could have affected the verdict one way or the other, jurors are allowed to use that fact any way they see fit. Including ordering major punitive damages.

So . . . *Go ahead and stonewall, guys,* was my attitude.

One thing had me stymied, though, as I went though the documents. All of the wrongful actions taken against my client—the memos that pressured him, the meetings where he was pressured, the decision to put him on PIP, and the final ultimatum, "You can resign or you'll be fired"—were, in fact, carried out by doctors. Every one of these people had "MD" after their name. So it appeared—as Coral Health claimed—that all these people *were* employed by the doctors' group, Triton. They *had* to be, because of California's rules against corporate practice of medicine, which forbade corporations from hiring doctors to practice medicine. Therefore, all the wrongful conduct was on Triton's part.

I knew that wasn't the case, though. I knew that the "edicts" issued to Triton doctors were coming from the top—from Coral—and so I knew there was something I was missing: a key to unlock this thing.

I strapped on my running shoes and hit the pavement again.

As I racked my brain about it, light finally dawned. I realized there were two distinct kinds of doctor in the picture here, though they all were technically MDs. One kind was the doctor who practiced medicine and actually saw patients. The other kind was the "medical director." They didn't *practice* medicine; they "managed" and "directed" it, hence their title. These were people who worked in offices and had no real interest in dealing with patients and little-to-no recent, real-world experience in medicine. And yet they routinely made treatment decisions for teams of highly experienced physicians who *were* up to date with all the latest modalities. But, again, it all *looked* medically kosher. On paper. If you didn't look too closely.

It hit me, as I was running along Balboa Island's South Bay Front, that in every instance, the doctors who engaged in the wrongful conduct toward my client had been medical *directors*, not practicing physicians. They *directed* medicine; they did not *practice* medicine. I knew this was a significant distinction.

It gave me an idea.

I did some more digging and requested more documents. Long story short, I found the key I had been looking for. The medical directors, although technically employed by Triton, were acting as "management and leadership" of Coral Health Partners, or so it appeared to me. Their paychecks were issued by Triton—follow the money!—but the funds for those paychecks came from Coral Health Partners (which, in turn, was part of Coral Health itself).

Ah, there it was: all of the "doctors" who were involved in forcing my client out of his job were "working" for Coral Health Partners! They had, in effect, been "installed" at Triton by Coral. I've since learned that medical directors are key players in the sleight of hand that allows corporations to operate medical facilities when the law expressly forbids the corporate practice of medicine.

74

Now I had just to officially tie the parent company in somehow. I knew that Coral Health was really the culprit. Its financial documents showed that it brought in $1.5 billion—yes, *billion*—a year from health insurance contracts. The fascinating thing was that all of this money was supposedly earmarked for "treating patients." But only doctors can treat patients. And as Coral Health informed me *ad nauseam*, it did not employ doctors. *So how was it treating patients, then?*

It was obvious to me that Coral Health was engaged in the very practice the law was designed to prevent—the corporate practice of medicine. Coral Health issued the policies governing doctors' behavior and handed those policies down to the physicians. The whole enterprise functioned like a single, connected company—like the big happy family its website boasted about. But Coral Health wanted to conveniently distance itself from that reality when the *bleep* hit the fan. I needed to find something that would show the court that the separation of these three entities was in name only.

I began to dig more deeply into the connection between the three entities and to ask more questions about it. I concluded I was on the right track, because as soon as I started to depose Coral Health and Coral Health Partners employees along these lines, suddenly no one knew anything. Suddenly, every question I asked was answered with "I don't know" or "I don't recall." High-level corporate lawyers started showing up at the depositions. Coral was getting nervous.

I finally discovered, deep in some e-mail chains, a couple of references to a document known as the System-Wide Memorandum of Understanding. Aha. Now that I had an official name for this document, I was able to demand that Coral Health produce it, and they weren't able to weasel out of giving it to me.

The System-Wide Memorandum of Understanding essentially showed that, for all intents and purposes, the Triton group was joined at the hip to Coral Health and had agreed to hew to all of its policies.

I was ready to argue my case.

But of course, Coral Health was not going to go quietly.

Every defendant in a lawsuit tries to have the suit dismissed without going to trial by using a "summary judgment motion." This is just what it sounds like—you try to force a judgment (in this case, a dismissal) in summary fashion (i.e., without going through a trial). Coral Health filed a summary judgment motion against us, and the judge denied it. He set a trial date, just three months out.

This was a huge victory for us. Scary, too. My client and I were going to put a major, well-known health-care system on trial. The story was front-page news, literally. The headline read "Doctor Sues Coral Health Medical Group" (of course, it used the company's real name, unlike I do here), along with the subheading "Alleges he was told to abide by illegal policies."

Two months out from trial, Coral Health made a final attempt to stop the trial and have the case dismissed. They appealed the judge's decision on the summary judgment motion. This is a highly unusual move—to try to appeal a decision to a higher court in the middle of a case. In my *particular* experience, however, it happens a lot. When the defendants finally realize they're going to court and see what's at stake, they often make a last-ditch effort to derail the train. Even if they lose the appeal—which they usually do—it delays the trial, which in itself can be a small victory for them. The longer a trial stretches out, the likelier it becomes that the plaintiff will give up or settle—or die, literally.

The defendants, of course, challenged my joint liability premise. This wasn't surprising. What *was* surprising was that the writ they filed accused the judge of *inventing* a *new* legal theory. To accuse a judge of inventing things—fabricating, essentially—was really audacious and, in my opinion, unwise. It's like calling a referee an idiot at the beginning of a game you're going to be playing. Coral Health was going to have to try its case in front of this same judge.

Whenever I see extreme behavior like this on the part of a defendant, I suspect I have struck a nerve and that they are behaving a bit desperately. I hoped this was the case here.

The defense's appeal was denied. The final hurdle had been removed, and it was time to go to trial.

PART IX

A Neurologist's Tale

The Trial

75

"Ladies and gentlemen of the jury," I say, launching into my opener. Hearing the words fall out of my mouth, I'm thinking to myself, *I sound like a broken record. This is the same opening I make in every case, with slight factual variations.* "The case you're about to hear is about money. My client is a neurologist who was employed by the defendants. The evidence will show that the defendants, in the interest of making money, created policies that negatively affected the way patient care was delivered. Evidence will also show that the defendants pressured my client to go along with these policies. And when my client resisted these policies, believing they were not good for his patients, my client was terminated in a damaging and retaliatory manner. You will hear the defense claim that my client wasn't actually terminated, but . . ."

I've probably used the exact same words in a dozen opening statements. That doesn't mean I'm lazy or passionless or that I'm "mailing it in." Not at all. Every time I say the words, I mean them freshly and wholeheartedly. And in every case, I care deeply about my client and the outcome. But there's no denying that a blueprint exists.

The reason my trials tend to fall into a pattern is that the *behavior of the insurance and health-care companies tends to fall into a pattern.* The pattern goes something like this: Company creates cost-saving policies that involve cutting corners on patient care. Conscientious doctor pushes back against policies. Company warns doctor to play ball. Doctor continues to push back. Company terminates doctor for phony reasons. Doctor sues company. Company covers its tracks.

The players change, and the details differ—in this particular case, for example, I'm suing a large health-care corporation instead of an insurance company—but the essential storyline remains the same. My job is simply to reveal that storyline to the jury.

In many ways, my most interesting work goes on during discovery and pretrial preparation as I try to find the hidden puzzle pieces that will bring the picture into view. But once I get to trial, there's an amazing amount of overlap with my other trials. I'm not saying, "If you've seen one of my trials, you've seen them all," but there is an almost "modular" feeling to the way my trials unfold. Certain "chunks" repeat themselves over and over. There are certain things I need to show the jury each and every time. These chunks comprise the building blocks of all my cases. Not every case contains every chunk, but there are patterns that run through all of my trial work.

In this case, the defense attorney's name is Gustafson. I've never seen him work, but I can almost hear his opening words before he says them.

"Ladies and gentlemen of the jury," Gustafson says, "this is not about a doctor who was wrongfully terminated. In fact, the evidence will show that this neurologist resigned of his own free will . . ."

As always, when the defense finishes its opening statement, I immediately request a copy of it, which I will now use as my game plan. During my closing arguments, I will try to debunk everything Gustafson has promised he's going to prove.

As always, I put my client on the stand first, so that the jury can get to know him and begin to feel a bond with him. That's not difficult with Bob Whalen. He comes off as extremely likeable and believable on the stand (as he does in person). I go through my standard questions, asking him about his background and the amount of time and effort that went into him becoming a doctor. Then we get into the why-we're-here-in-court stuff.

"When did you begin having disagreements with your employer, Dr. Whalen?"

"After Coral Health purchased the company. It began issuing policies that I did not believe were good for patient care," replies Bob.

"Can you tell us about some of those policies?"

"They wanted us to see patients for shorter appointments and at less frequent intervals. They wanted us to prescribe only cheaper medications that were on a preapproved list. They wanted to severely limit the number of tests we ordered for patients and the number of referrals we wrote. They wanted us to spend more of our patient time on record keeping."

"And what was your reaction to these policy changes?"

"I spoke up against them. I continued to prescribe the medications I believed were best for my patient, not just those on the preapproved list. I continued to spend a clinically appropriate amount of time with my patients. I referred them for tests and additional treatments if I thought such things were indicated."

"Did that behavior become an issue for you, in terms of your relationship with the defendant?"

"Yes. I began to receive e-mails and memos from the administration, telling me that my treatment practices were out of sync with the company's policies. There were a couple of meetings where I was told, point blank, to become more of a 'team player.' Eventually, I was ordered to resign or face harshly punishing measures."

"And why did you decide to sue Coral Health nearly two years after leaving its employment?"

"I learned that some of my former patients were being medically harmed by the policies my former employer was enforcing. One of them nearly died, but I intervened on his behalf. Also, I knew that many of my peers were being pressured the same way I was and that they were struggling with deep moral dilemmas."

Again, you could almost copy and paste much of Bob's testimony into the transcripts of a half dozen of my other trials. That's not a slam on Bob; he testified beautifully. The slam is on the systematic and repetitive abuses I see in the health-care system. And in order to show those systematic abuses to juries, I need to lead them through several predictable steps at trial.

I need to show them how the company made its money and how the company's policies were designed to increase the bottom line rather than improve patient care. I need to show them that my client practiced sound medicine and was a "good doctor." I need to show them that my client was pressured into doing things that went against his or her best medical judgment. I need to show them that when my client resisted the company's cost-cutting measures, he or she was flagged as a problem employee. I need to show them that, eventually, my client was given an ultimatum: shape up, quit, or be fired. Et cetera, et cetera.

This particular case fits pretty cleanly into the pattern. And since you've already seen the details play out in a couple of other trials, I won't do a blow by blow of all the steps.

76

Of course, every case has its surprises and its unique twists and turns, too. And in that regard, this case was no different.

For example, it took a crazily long time to get through jury selection. That was because almost everyone in the city where the trial was held received their health care from Coral Health through one of its "affiliated" medical groups—not just Triton, but several others as well. That fact didn't bother me, but it sure bothered the defendants. They did *not* want to seat any jurors who'd had experience with Coral Health, and they used up all their peremptory challenges toward that end. (I thought this was a mistake. The message they were clearly sending was that anyone who'd had experience with Coral Health would, by definition, have a negative attitude toward the company.)

Looking back on this case, there were a couple of key moments that stood out in the testimony phase and gave the case its unique flavor. One of these occurred during the plaintiff's case, the other during the defense's case.

"Leakage" was a major issue at Coral Health and was one of the key concepts the administration used to get its physicians to follow its new policies. A crucial part of my cases involves trying, through testimony pulled from hostile witnesses, to get the jury to understand what seemingly innocuous industry terms like "leakage" really mean. Once the jury "gets" these concepts, it's as if a veil has been lifted.

In this case, I had an incredibly powerful exhibit that I couldn't wait to show the jury. It came out during the testimony of one of Coral Health's medical directors, Dr. Byrd.

"Will you tell the jury what your role is at Coral Health, Dr. Byrd?"

"I write policies and procedures governing physicians' activities, and I help enforce those policies on a day-to-day basis."

"Do your policies affect the way staff physicians practice medicine?"

"Yes, I am responsible for a number of policies that impact member care."

"When you use the word 'members,' do you mean 'patients'?"

"Well, yes."

"Interesting choice of words. It's almost as if you think of them in terms of money first."

"Objection."

"Sustained. Careful, Ms. Barta."

"Are you familiar with the industry term 'leakage'?" I asked Byrd.

"Yes."

"Can you tell us what the word 'leakage' means in health-care parlance?"

"Yes; it refers to money a health-care system loses by referring patients to physicians and other providers outside the system."

"Leakage is considered a bad thing by your employer, is it not?"

"Well, it certainly isn't good. Not from a business perspective."

"One of your roles is to help your employer control leakage, is it not?"

"You could say that."

"And you accomplish that by—among other things—discouraging doctors from making outside referrals, is that correct?"

"We are always looking for ways we can provide more comprehensive member care under our own umbrella."

"Did you instruct a Coral Health employee to create this document?"

At this point, I entered the PowerPoint document called "Leakage"—remember that one?—into evidence and displayed it on the overhead screen. The audience and jury literally gasped when they saw the cover picture of a sewage-filled public bathroom.

"Yes, I did," said Byrd, a bit reluctantly.

"Would you agree, Dr. Byrd, that the cover of this document equates money spent on patient care with raw human waste?"

"The document refers to money spent *unnecessarily* on patient care—outside the system!"

"But sometimes, when practicing good medicine," I said, "it *is* necessary to refer a patient to an outside specialist, is it not?"

"Sometimes."

"And, in your opinion, who should make the decision as to when a patient needs to receive medical services not available under Coral Health's umbrella?"

"Ideally, the treating physician," he answered.

"But when Bob Whalen made such decisions, he got in trouble, did he not?"

"He was making too many referrals. He was being . . . wasteful."

I was headed back to the plaintiffs' table when I heard this word pop out of his mouth. I stopped in my tracks and spun around on my heel to face him.

"I'm sorry, Dr. Byrd, could you repeat that last word one more time?"

"Objection," said Gustafson. "The jury heard it the first time."

"Sustained."

But Byrd said it anyway. "Wasteful."

I paused, looked meaningfully at the photo of the waste-filled bathroom, and then looked back at Byrd's reddening face. I decided to let the word hang in the air like the foul odor that the picture suggested.

"No further questions, Your Honor."

As I headed back to my table, I glanced at the jury. They were staring at the photo in something resembling shock.

77

The other key moment happened during the defense's presentation. It, too, was a proplaintiff moment. Now, you might legitimately point out that I'm only showing the moments that went well for our side—that's a fair criticism to which I freely plead guilty—but this one really was a "movie moment." I feel compelled to include it because it shows the kinds of lows to which defense teams can sometimes sink when their backs are against the wall.

The defense's final witness was a Mr. Andrew Larsen. He was a surprise "rebuttal" witness, not on the original witness list. After being sworn in, Larsen testified that he worked in the Grievance and Appeals arm of Coral Health's HR department.

Attorney Gustafson addressed the court reporter, asking her to read aloud a section of Bob Whalen's testimony where he claimed to have received no patient-care complaints in all of his time at Triton.

When the reading was complete, Gustafson turned to Larsen and said, "What is your reaction to hearing that testimony by the plaintiff?"

"It's not true," said Andrew Larsen.

"Why do you say that?"

"Because my department did, in fact, receive several complaints from patients about this doctor, citing a number of unprofessional behaviors."

"Such as?"

"Treating patients rudely, keeping them waiting excessively long times in examining rooms, failing to explain procedures adequately, yelling at nurses and assistants in front of patients, refusing to listen to patients . . ."

The complaints went on. I was in shock—these behaviors sounded nothing like the Bob Whalen I knew and respected. But they were having their desired effect: making my client seem horrible to the jury. Something fishy was going on here, but what was it? A memory began tickling the back of my mind, but I couldn't quite tease it to the foreground. It had something to do with this witness's last name. What was it, damn it? I had the sense it was important, whatever it was. Critical, even.

Oh well; I couldn't waste any more mental energy on it. I needed to focus on the task at hand: challenging the witness on these phony-sounding complaints. When it was my turn to cross-examine Larsen, I asked him, "Do you have any records documenting these alleged complaints by patients about my client?"

"I have records, yes . . . on my computer."

"On your computer?"

"That's right."

"And did you bring your computer along today?"

"No, I didn't."

"Well, then, did you print out these alleged complaints from your computer?"

"No."

"Why not?"

"I didn't feel it was necessary. I've read the complaints, and I can recall what they said."

"*You* can recall, but what about the rest of us? You didn't feel it was important to bring along *any written records* to support these claims? Why not? You didn't think anyone would be interested in a trifling detail such as hard evidence?"

"Objection," said Gustafson. "Badgering."

"Sustained," said the judge. "Careful, Counsel."

I turned back to the witness and stared at him, awaiting his response.

"I was called on short notice," he said. "I didn't have time to make printouts."

"But evidently you had time to go back to your computer and *review* these complaints. Or are we to believe you have them memorized from over two years ago?"

The witness began stammering to come up with an answer. I let this go on for a few seconds, then turned to the judge and said, "Your Honor, I *could* ask this witness to come back tomorrow and produce all the documents he claims to have 'on his computer,' but I don't want to delay this trial any longer." I looked at the witness and said, "So I'm going to take your word for the fact that these complaints are real, Mr. Larsen. I guess we'll all have to. It'll just be your word and your credibility."

I repeated, "Your credibility," one last time, looking at the jury, and headed back to the plaintiffs' table. As I was taking those few short steps, the memory suddenly hit me, the one that had been poking at me during his testimony:

During discovery, I had seen numerous documents signed by Coral Health's in-house attorney, Nancy Arroyo (who happened to be present in court today). In most of those documents, she used the name Arroyo, but in a few of them, she had signed her name differently. Like me, she used her maiden name as her professional handle, but her married name was different.

I was struck by a hunch—a strong one—but I didn't know whether I should play it. If I played it and was wrong, I would look like an idiot. But if I was right. . .

My intuition was telling me to go for it.

Oh well: no guts, no glory.

I turned back to Larsen and said, "I do have one last question, Mr. Larsen. How did you come to testify today?"

"I was subpoenaed."

"Really?" I said. "Someone handed you a legal summons."

"I don't recall."

"Well, you just said you were called on short notice. Surely you would remember if, within the last twenty-four hours, someone had handed you a legal document requiring you to show up in court?"

"But I don't," he said, his frayed nerves showing. "I don't remember."

I wasn't buying it, and neither was the jury.

"You don't remember, Mr. Larsen, because it didn't happen," I said. "What happened was that someone personally *asked* you to testify, isn't that right?"

Pause.

"Yes," he admitted reluctantly.

"And who was that person?"

"Attorney Arroyo," he said, pointing at the in-house counsel, seated at the defense table.

"And you know Attorney Arroyo personally, don't you?"

"Yes."

"What's her married name?"

At this point, the jury's heads were moving back and forth between Larsen, Arroyo, and me, as if they were watching a tennis match.

"It's Larsen. Nancy Larsen."

"Attorney Larsen is your wife, isn't she?"

"Yes," mutters Andrew Larsen.

"I'm sorry, Mr. Larsen, we didn't quite catch that. Can you repeat your answer?"

"Yes."

"As I said, we'll be relying on your credibility. No more questions."

78

The case (that is, the evidence part of it) has finally concluded, and closing arguments have been made. Bob and I are now waiting in the courtroom hallway for the verdict. I think I'm more nervous than he is. I'm feeling good about how the case has gone but uncertain as to how the jury will lean. A lot depends on whether they agree with my argument that this is a case of "constructive termination." As I've mentioned, it's a higher bar to hit. There is no doubt that Bob resigned from Triton—no one is disputing that. The question is whether his resignation was truly voluntary or whether Coral Health had made his work situation so hostile that it amounted to a constructive termination.

We finally get the word that the jury has reached a verdict.

We file into the courtroom.

Long story short, the judge announces that the jury has found for the plaintiff—Bob—regarding wrongful termination. Bob clasps his hands together as if in prayer, and I know it's for his patients and colleagues that he's feeling victorious. The judge then informs us that the jury has awarded economic damages in the exact amount we had asked for and has also voted for punitive damages.

As typically happens, the judge orders the jury to return in two days in order to conduct its deliberations as to the amount of the punitive damages.

And here's the final way this case plays out a bit unusually. The defense lawyers don't offer to settle; they just quietly exit the courtroom. As I've mentioned before, the defense usually prefers to avoid having the jury decide on the amount of punitive damages. But in this case, they've apparently decided to let the cards fall where they will. Maybe it's because they believe that, despite the verdict, they've got a prodefense jury. Maybe they feel that because Bob quit voluntarily, the punitive damages will be light. Or maybe they feel they have grounds for appeal. Maybe none of the above. I have no idea.

Whatever the reason, the punitive damages will be up to the jury.

At the hearing for punitive damages, both the defense attorney and I are allowed to address the jury before they start their deliberations. Here's where I trot out the final piece of my "prefab" script. It's a spiel that has worked for me in the past, and I don't believe in messing with success. So I dust it off and use it today.

"Ladies and gentlemen of the jury," I say, "I have teenage daughters. If one of them does something wrong, I'm going to punish her, and I want that punishment to be fair. But I also want it to be . . . felt. And remembered. So I look into her piggy bank, and let's say I find a hundred dollars there. I want her to pay an amount that will make her feel some pain and think twice about misbehaving again. So what do we think that amount should be? Five dollars? Nah, no real pain there, right? Not when she has a hundred dollars in the bank. That's only a caramel macchiato, small. Ten dollars? Probably still not enough. What about fifty? Whoa. That's probably too much; I don't want to break her.

"How about twenty-something dollars? Hmm, now we're in the range where she's going to feel some pain but hasn't been wiped out financially. That's the kind of thinking I encourage you to use when you're deciding on a figure for punitive damages. You don't want to wipe the defendants out, but you want to discourage them from engaging in this kind of behavior in the future."

After giving my piggy-bank analogy, I present the defendants' balance sheets. In this case, I show the jurors that the amount of money Coral Health has "in the bank" as pure profit—not as operating budget, mind you, but pure profit—its in the hundreds of millions of dollars. And then I turn them loose with their calculators and wish them luck.

The jury comes back with a huge punitive award. All things considered, it's beyond fair, in my opinion, and my client is extremely happy. The defense, however, does not look similarly pleased.

The nice part about not accepting a settlement is that we can now talk publicly about the case. Newspapers and media will report the verdict and the jury awards, and my client can talk freely to the press. He'll also get to speak publicly about holding health-care companies accountable for the human costs of their decisions. Best of all, maybe Coral Health, and other companies like it, will think twice before brazenly putting greed and profits ahead of patients and their health care.

At least we can say we gave it our best shot.

Part X

Outcomes

79

In case you're wondering how things turned out for our three doctors . . .

The Psychiatrist

After receiving a multimillion dollar verdict and settlement, Dr. Han ultimately retired. But first, he hired a younger psychiatrist who shared his practice philosophy. He worked with his patients to gradually transition their care to their new doctor. Dr. Han moved into a beautiful new home with his wife and now splits his time between playing and traveling with his grandchildren and continuing his pro bono work.

The Dermatologist

In addition to receiving financial restoration, Dr. Mangini became recontracted with all of the insurance companies, was removed from prepayment review (PPR), and was able to move forward as a physician. All of her patients received letters informing them that she was now "in network," which led them back to her practice. She started a family, and her practice continues to grow. She still fights back whenever an insurance company tries a new tactic that she believes is not in the best interests of patients (her own or any doctor's).

The Neurologist

After his vindication in court, Dr. Whalen's "concierge" practice thrived. He joined up with several other doctors to create a new kind of medical group. This innovative group employs a payment model that just might be the wave of the future. In essence, the doctors themselves act as the "insurer." Each patient pays the group a set amount per year, and the doctors provide all necessary medical care for that set price. The patients love it because they can see the doctor of *their* choice *when*ever they want. The doctors love it because they receive enough income to run their practice successfully. And, most importantly, no one needs to deal with those greedy profits-before-patients insurance companies.

My Closing Argument

Every time I try a case, I hope that the verdict will sound an alarm within the health-care system and that the defendant—insurance company, medical group, or management company—will "change its evil ways." I'm not naïve enough to believe that that actually happens most of the time, but I do know that some of my cases *have* done some good. I see this when a new case unfolds and I learn that a corrupt practice or policy that I brought to light in a previous case is no longer being employed.

The frustrating thing I continue to grapple with is that the abusive practices highlighted in this book are rampant in our country, and few people know about them. I hope this book will help to change that. I hope it will bring to light the fact that our doctors—whom we desperately need, especially as our population ages—are being treated like devalued pawns in today's world of corporate medicine. Doctors need our support, not our anger and resentment.

The simple fact is that when doctors are mistreated by insurers and employers and "hobbled" in their medical practices, patients are the ones who ultimately suffer. A doctor who is pressured by corporate policy to double- and triple-book his appointments, see more patients in a day than can possibly be treated thoughtfully, prescribe only preapproved (read: cheap) medications, and deny as many services as possible is not able to give his or her patients the quality care they expect and deserve. And when a doctor is fired unfairly, it is the doctor's patients who lose a valued partner in their health care.

Patients—i.e., all of us—need to educate ourselves. We need to be aware that there are not only laws that protect doctors from retaliation but also medical principles that safeguard patients' rights and protect their ability to receive health care without interference from insurers and health-care systems. For example, here are some provisions of the AMA (American Medical Association) Principles for Physician Employment:

> "Patient advocacy is a fundamental element of the patient-physician relationship that should not be altered by the health care system or setting in which physicians practice."

> "Termination of an employment or contractual relationship between a physician and an entity employing the physician does not necessarily end the patient-physician relationship between the physician and persons under his or her care. When a physician's employment status is unilaterally terminated by an employer, the physician and his or her employer should notify the physician's patients that the physician will no longer by working with the employer and should provide them with the physician's new contact information."[1]

Though insurers and health-care providers don't like to talk about this anymore, the patient–physician relationship is sacrosanct. And because of that, patients have a right to what is called "continuity of care." This means that if you learn that your doctor has left, or is leaving, your medical group, you have the *right* to know where your

---

1 American Medical Association, *AMA Principles for Physician Employment*, 2013, http://www.ncmedsoc.org/wp-content/uploads/2013/09/ama-principles-for-physician-employment.pdf.

physician is going and to receive their new contact information. It is also your *right* to continue to be seen by your current doctor in his or her new practice or transfer your care to another physician within the present group. If someone at your medical group tells you they can't give you that information because it's confidential or feeds you a line that sounds fishy or made up, don't accept it. You have rights, and you have legal recourse if those rights are being ignored.

Again, bottom line: it is the *patient's* choice whom they see as their doctor. And if we, as patients, want to be able to choose doctors who put our interests first and who give us the kind of care we desire, then we need to step up and speak out for them. Your doctor's main responsibility is to *you*, and most doctors wouldn't want it any other way. The Code of Medical Ethics, based on the Hippocratic oath, states, "A physician must recognize responsibility to patients first and foremost, as well as to society, other health professionals, and to self." Nowhere in this code are insurance companies mentioned.

It used to be that doctors owned their medical practices or medical groups, employed their own staff and nurses, owned or leased their own buildings and equipment, and collected the monies due them for their services, either directly from patients or from the insurance companies. That meant that, in essence, the doctors "ran the show" and were able to practice medicine the way their medical judgment dictated, without interference from corporate interests. That arrangement was healthy for both doctors and patients. But all of that has been flipped on its head. Nowadays, insurance companies and the "management" groups they partner with own the buildings and equipment, employ the staff and nurses, and control the flow of money that doctors collect and receive for their services. Through their control of the purse strings, these corporations are also controlling our doctors' professional activities and the type of care they are able to offer us as patients. Money, for the most part, runs medicine.

The simple fact is that profit and patient care don't go together. This system has a built-in conflict of interest. We now find ourselves in a position where patient *care* is dwindling and patient *costs* are going up, while insurers and health-care systems are reaping record profits and their top executives are earning truly mind-blowing salaries. CEOs of for-profit health systems and insurance companies now make $15 million *a year* and more in salaries and bonuses—in one case, $22 million! Meanwhile, patients are paying huge and ever-increasing premiums, with large deductibles and copays, as well as paying out of pocket for many "noncovered" services. What many people don't seem to realize is that denial of patient care is the very engine that drives these corporations' profits. Every medical service or procedure an insurer approves means money *out* of its pocket; every medical service or procedure it denies means money *in* its pockets. It's really as simple as that. The greed of insurance companies and their executives is going largely unchecked, and the "for-profit" model is turning patient care into a contracted service provided by the lowest bidder, like carpet cleaning or package delivery.

The day is coming soon—in fact, it is already here—when we must ask ourselves, as a people and a nation, the fundamental question: Who do we really want in charge of our health care? Those interested in our *health* or those interested in our *money*?

About the Author

Theresa Barta is a physician's advocate. She started her law practice in 1998 and has since represented hundreds of physicians in litigation matters against insurance companies, medical groups, and HMOs. She tried one of the first cases in California under the state's anti-retaliation statute and has won many multimillion-dollar verdicts and settlements for her clients. In 2013, she was named Top Gun Trial Lawyer of the Year.

Ms. Barta began her career with the law firm of Morrison & Foerster, where she specialized in business litigation, and from there went on to work for Shernoff Bidart Echeverria, where she litigated cases in the firm's health-insurance practice—in particular, bad-faith disputes against health insurers and HMOs.

She is admitted to practice in the United States Supreme Court, US Courts of Appeal for the Ninth and Eleventh Circuits, and all of the state and federal courts in California. She holds a JD from Loyola Law School, where she graduated Order of the Coif and was a member of the St. Thomas More Law Honor Society.

Ms. Barta lives in Newport Beach, California, with her husband and has two daughters.